LONDON TRANSPORT
in the 1980s

Michael H. C. Baker

Contents

Introduction	… … … … …	3
1.	Political Decisions … … … …	5
2.	Jubilee No 1: Green Line … … …	10
3.	London Country in the Early 1980s … …	13
4.	Underground Downs and Ups … … …	30
5.	Jubilee No 2: London Transport … …	36
6.	Some Good Things Come to an End … …	44
7.	Varying Fortunes — The Routemaster and the DMS	54
8.	The London Regional Transport Act … …	62
9.	Travel for the Disabled, and the Hoppa … …	66
10.	The New 'Red Bus' Companies … … …	70
11.	The Tube, the King's Cross Fire and the Docklands Light Railway … …	74
12.	Privatisation … … … … …	84
Bibliography	… … … … …	96

First published 2008

ISBN 978 0 7110 3283 5

All rights reserved. No part of this book may be reproduced or transmitted in any form or by any means, electronic or mechanical, including photocopying, recording or by any information storage and retrieval system, without permission from the Publisher in writing.

© Michael H. C. Baker 2008

Published by Ian Allan Publishing

an imprint of Ian Allan Publishing Ltd, Hersham, Surrey, KT12 4RG

Printed in England by Ian Allan Printing Ltd, Hersham, Surrey, KT12 4RG

Code: 0809/B1

Visit the Ian Allan Publishing website at www.ianallanpublishing.com

Introduction

TUESDAY 1 January 1980 was a far less significant date than New Year's Day 1970, when what had been the Country Area of London Transport — the green buses and Green Line coaches — was hived off to the National Bus Company. Huge changes had taken place in the intervening 10 years, and not much was left to remind passengers in East Grinstead, Luton, Slough, Tilbury etc that their towns had once been a very large part of the empire administered since 1933 from Holden's handsome 55 Broadway, close neighbour of St James's Park, Westminster Abbey and the Houses of Parliament. Which does not mean, dear reader, that we will no longer take account of the story of public transport as experienced by our country cousins in the 1980s. Whilst my formative years had been spent travelling by tram, trolleybus, petrol/diesel bus and Underground train, during the latter part of the 1960s and through most of the 1970s, I had become one of those country cousins. Now, in the 1980s, I was for the first time living permanently beyond even the furthest-reaching tentacle of London Transport. Strictly speaking this is not absolutely true. Discarded members of the DMS class ran past our front door in

Wareham for 10 years, whilst others, still officially domiciled at 55 Broadway, regularly appeared at summer weekends in Dorset, after we had moved there, hired by LT staff and their families for a day beside the sea.

Some years earlier, when teaching at a secondary school in South Norwood, I had been momentarily taken aback one Monday morning when, on enquiring about what 12-year-old Winston had done at the weekend, I learned he had gone to the seaside 'on a number 12 bus', until I remembered his Dad was a conductor at Elmers End garage.

Many of the inhabitants of the small, historic market town (with the only intact Saxon earth walls in the land) to which we had moved, had also come from the London area and declared: 'We're never going back'. Setting aside the fact that property prices made a permanent return impossible anyhow, unless one were prepared to settle for a large shed in the less fashionable areas of, say Upminster or Crouch End, I took — and still take — the opposite view, and if more than a couple of weeks go by without a trip back to 'The Smoke' I get the most terrible withdrawal symptoms. Driving up, I can be parked

Two Routemasters, RM1738 leading RM1846, keep each other company on route 11 in a momentarily quiet Whitehall on 12 February 1981. *Graham Smith*

3

A Leyland Titan heads across the Thames by way of Waterloo Bridge in October 1989, the picture dominated by the steamer *Queen Mary* and, in the background, Somerset House. Built on the Clyde by Denny Bros in 1935, the *Queen Mary* became the *Queen Mary II* when the somewhat larger Cunard liner of the same name entered service, and since 1988 has been a floating restaurant on the Thames, her original name restored.

in Richmond or by Kew Gardens in 110 minutes — I once made it to Covent Garden early one Sunday morning in precisely two hours — whilst the hourly through service from our local station gets us to Waterloo in just over two hours.

London, it need hardly be said, is unique. It may not be the most beautiful capital city in the world (Edinburgh and Prague score there), and it may not be as stylish as Paris or as spectacular as New York (yes, I know that's actually not the American capital, merely the world's capital), but even if I'm not quite a Londoner (having been born some seven and a half miles south of Charing Cross, in Croydon, makes me a native of Surrey) it's still *my* city, the one I know better than any other. Among the most significant contributions to London's uniqueness are its big red double-deckers. This statement may now, towards the end of the first decade of the 21st century, be almost a cliché, but it is nevertheless true. I have always known it. I have known it since the first time, sitting at the front of what I called a 'long tram', years before I learned its correct title was a 'Feltham', as we rounded the curve by the Archbishop of Canterbury's Palace and clattered over Lambeth Bridge, there was the breathtaking spectacle of the Thames, Big Ben and the whole panorama of London spread before me. Hadn't Mrs Edwards, our head teacher, informed us that this was the capital of the greatest empire the world had ever seen, and that we, little English boys and girls, were the luckiest people on the planet? We never for a moment doubted her.

By the time I was nine I had met John Wadham and Clive Gillam in class 5, Winterbourne Primary School, London SW25 (I still correspond with the latter on the other side of the world), proud owners of the first edition of the Ian Allan 'ABCs' of London's buses, trams, trolleybuses and trains, and who let me into the secrets of 'E1s', STLs, the Tolworth Loop and the Inner Circle. Long before I acquired an Irish wife, to say nothing of a part Chinese/Thai grandson, I began to question whether the view that Mrs Edwards (and the *Daily Mail*, delivered to our house each day) took of the world was wholly correct. But I'm not sure that I have ever quite relinquished the notion Clive, John and I assumed some 60 years ago: that London had a public-transport system as good as any in the world. Oh yes, I know it's far from perfect, that No 11s still arrive in bunches, that the Northern Line will decide to shut down in the heart of the rush hour, that 'they keep putting the fares up', that one's fellow passengers push and shove, 'not like in the old days', etc, etc, etc, but in truth it was ever thus. One tries to avoid turning into a 'grumpy old man', Victor Meldrew-style, but few things annoy me more than enthusiasts who long for the days when 'there used to be real buses' (meaning, I suppose, purpose-built half-cabs with conductors), ignoring the fact that the modern London bus is comfortable, frequent, less polluting and has a huge capacity, and that the best of them are some of the most elegant PSVs ever seen. If that's not real, I don't know what is.

Michael H. C. Baker
Wareham, Dorset
July 2008

• 1 •

Political Decisions

THE 1980s was a funny old time. Fashion was whatever you wanted it to be, whilst, to quote *The Independent*, in the world of pop music (which to much of youth appeared to be the only one which counted), 'The accent was on amateurism, neo-romanticism and unashamed artifice, whether as an ironic commentary on the business of pop or as a celebration of its flimsy surfaces', and classical music, with the rise of the minimalists, Glass, Reich and Adams, and the extraordinarily popular composer of religious music, John Tavener, was turning back to pleasing instead of alienating audiences. This was the decade when politics raised its ugly/pretty (delete as appropriate) head and became more intimately involved in public transport than at any time since the setting up of London Transport in 1933.

The Conservative Prime Minister, Margaret Thatcher, declared that there was no such thing as society and is also alleged to have remarked that 'any young man above the age of 26 seen riding on a bus has not succeeded in life'. Whether she really did say this, and whether the age quoted was 26, 30 or 40, has been hotly debated ever since. Whether LOTS, the London Bus Preservation Trust and the Friends of the London Transport Museum immediately offered her membership of their respective — and, indeed, highly respectable — organisations, in order to persuade her of the error of her ways, I cannot say. Certainly such a remark, (if it was made), seen from 20 years on, leaves one simply gasping with incredulity.

There is no doubt that the Thatcher era was far from a golden one for public transport. Ken Livingstone, in 1981 elected Leader of the Greater London Council, together with Sir Peter Masefield, Chair of the London Transport Executive, brought in a measure — 'Fares Fair' — to cut fares by 25% and even talked of free transport in the capital. Practically no-one doubted that car travel in London had to be controlled if gridlock were not to ensue, and therefore people had to be persuaded, encouraged, coerced or whatever to desert their cars for buses and trains. The GLC also introduced the 'Travelcard' (subsequently adopted in one form or another by cities all over the world), which allowed the public to buy unlimited daily or weekly travel. As a consequence bus and Underground travel shot up, but the Conservative Government, mindful of its electoral promise to rein in public spending, reduced the GLC's transport grant by £119 million. The Conservative-controlled Bromley Council, on the south-eastern fringes of London, claimed it was unfair that it should have to contribute to a scheme of little benefit to the majority of its ratepayers and took the GLC to court. Bromley lost the first round in the divisional court but won on appeal. The final judgement, in the House of Lords on 17 December 1981, was against the GLC.

In 1982, with the 'Fares Fair' scheme still in operation, car usage in London dropped by 10%, bus usage rose by 14% and Underground usage by a staggering 44% — the greatest increases in the 49-year history of London Transport. An independent survey discovered that 71% of Londoners were in favour of subsidised public transport. But the law had to be obeyed, and in the new year fares were generally doubled, 1,253 London Transport jobs were lost, 500 buses were taken out of service, car travel increased again, and (it is estimated) the number of serious road accidents rose by 6,000. Another consequence was the first scheduled withdrawals of Routemasters, although it would be two decades before normal service of the type in London came to an end. A little earlier, in 1980, the delightful phenomenon of the 'Showbus' emerged, a number of garages lavishing tender loving care on a selected vehicle (usually a Routemaster), embellishing it in various, often quite subtle ways, sending it off to rallies and keeping it in tip-top condition. This was another demonstration of how many London bus people regarded their profession not merely as a job but as a consuming passion. The political changes of the early 1980s did nothing to encourage them, the loss being not just theirs but that of the travelling public in general.

5

London Transport had been acquiring second-hand Routemasters since the mid-1970s, the first being the forward-entrance airport buses released by British Airways from 1975. These had been used briefly in passenger service but were employed chiefly as driver trainers and staff buses, functions they were still performing at the beginning of the 1980s. In 1979/80 came 12 more forward-entrance Routemasters, this time from Northern General, the only undertaking outside London to buy new Routemasters. For all sorts of reasons, most centred around union resistance and the need for costly modifications, these never entered ordinary service with London Transport, although some worked the Round London Sightseeing Tour, an increasingly popular feature and one at which other operators were looking enviously. As the climate in Britain seemed to grow milder throughout the 1980s and the winters less severe, so the open-top bus, which it seemed had gone for ever from the streets of London some 50 years earlier, began to reappear in increasing numbers and in a variety of forms. By the end of the decade London Buses Ltd had lost its monopoly, and competition would become ever fiercer in the years to come.

Above: The Showbus phenomenon of the early 1980s is typified by RM1000 sparkling in the spring sunshine of 1981 as it overtakes National LS87 near Broad Green, Croydon. The Routemaster is a real credit to the staff at Croydon garage.

Left: One of many non-standard Routemasters acquired by London Transport was one-time BEA forward-entrance 'coach' RMA5. Used for a short period in 1975/6 on passenger work from Romford garage, it is seen here at King's Cross on driver-training duty, the (forward) staircase having been removed to accommodate an instructor's seat immediately behind the driver.

Above: A remarkable type to appear on the Round London Sightseeing Tour was the BMMO D9. Designed 'in house' by the company, few Midland Red buses entered the second-hand market, but a number of these unusual vehicles, the last Midland Red-designed and -built double-deckers to go into production, had their roofs removed and were adapted for London use. This one is seen negotiating Hyde Park Corner in 1982.

Below: Also used on sightseeing duties in the early 1980s were seven ex-Bournemouth Transport Weymann-bodied Daimler Fleetlines dating from 1965 and acquired by LT in 1978. These were particularly suitable in that they were fitted with removable roofs, having performed seafront duties in the summer with their original owner. Seen in March 1980 at Waterloo, with roofs firmly in place, are DMO1 (named *Stockwell Princess* by its home garage) and DMO4.

Two vastly less-successful types which disappeared in the early 1980s were the Merlin and Swift. These final, sad, Southall-built single-deckers provided a swansong to a long and otherwise honourable tradition, AEC having been the major supplier of London's buses for the best part of a century. Some saw service elsewhere, and several have, quite rightly, been preserved, for they are very much part of the story of the London bus. A few of the longer and more powerful Merlins, assisted latterly by some of the shorter Swifts, lasted on Red Arrow service into early 1981, by which time the older examples had long since disappeared elsewhere. The last non-Red Arrow Swift, SMS771, ended its career on 23 January 1981, at Edgware garage, whilst in the spring and early summer Leyland National 2s, built at Workington, gradually took over Red Arrow work, establishing a monopoly by the end of July.

Above: LT's last Swifts were taken out of service in the summer of 1981. One of the last survivors was Edgware's SMS376, seen here heading through Watford on the 142. DMSs would take over by early December 1980, and SMS376 would be sold to Wombwell Diesels for scrap in January 1981.

The contest between Margaret Thatcher, the 'Iron Lady', and 'Red Ken' Livingstone was one which gripped Londoners and intrigued (even amused) others, especially those standing on the sidelines who would be unaffected by the outcome. Livingstone had the figures of unemployed, then steadily rising, displayed in neon lights on County Hall, facing the Houses of Parliament across the Thames. Thatcher was incandescent, her response being to ensure the abolition not only of the 'Fares Fair' scheme but of the GLC itself. Before this, on 29 June 1984, the GLC

Above: Two shiny new Leyland National 2s (LS500 nearer the camera) on Red Arrow duties at Waterloo in the summer of 1981.

Ash Grove Garage

Opening Ceremony
Tuesday 21 April 1981

LONDON BUSES TOWER DISTRICT **Going places**

lost control of London Transport when London Regional Transport was set up, and the day-to-day operation of the capital's buses became the responsibility of London Buses Ltd. Driver-only operation, it was announced, would have to reach 75% by 1988, by which time the staff would be reduced by 3,800, and LRT would put bus services out to competitive tender, on the basis that, in every case, the cheapest bid should be accepted.

Despite losing these battles, it can be said that, in the long term, Ken Livingstone won the war. He became an MP, and although he was not exactly a favourite of the Labour leader, Tony Blair (at one stage even being expelled from the Labour Party), the creation — ironically by the 1997 Labour Government — of the office of Mayor of London enabled him to run for this elected office as an independent. Duly elected in May 2000, he gained unprecented control over the capital's public transport, and in 2004, having been readmitted to the Labour fold, won a second term.

Above: Another garage to receive an allocation of new Leyland National 2s for Red Arrow work was Ash Grove, opened in April 1981 to replace Hackney and Dalston. Political machinations would force its closure after just 10 years .

Jubilee No 1: Green Line

GREEN Line was registered as a company on 9 July 1930 by LGOC and thus celebrated its Golden Jubilee in the summer of 1980. It was established chiefly to combat the competition from a host of operators which, since the late 1920s, had been operating express services from the Home Counties and the outer suburbs to Central London. These took customers away not only from the mainly steam-operated railways (at least, those north of the Thames) but also from the longer-distance bus routes. To quote from the Golden Jubilee issue of the Green Line Coach Guide, issued in the summer of 1980, 'as licensing was entirely in the hands of local authorities, there was little co-ordination; many roads had several different companies vying for business along them'. The names were colourful and evocative — Premier Line, Acme (no, not acne, although one or two of the smaller operators were scarcely out of their teens), Skylark, Strawhatter (from Luton) … but no Cabinet Maker from High Wycombe. 'The new coaches were comfortable, convenient and cheap.

They stopped anywhere you wanted, and a cheap day return from London to Windsor, for instance, left you change from 3/6d (17½p)'.

The LGOC and its associates, East Surrey and National, which operated north of the Thames, were not slow to get in on the act; an express department was formed in 1928, and by the end of 1931 Green Line was operating no fewer than 275 coaches on 27 different routes. The livery chosen was quite superb: sage-green lower panels, black waistband, grey window frames, another black band and a silver roof. Fortunately T219 of 1930 is preserved in the London Transport collection in its original state.

The Golden Jubilee issue of the Green Line Coach Guide for the summer of 1980 lists 31 routes. Most were hourly, some operated only at rush hours, and three were seasonal. There were several significant changes in pattern, not just since the 1930s but since the early-postwar boom in bus and coach travel. Increasing traffic congestion meant that routes which previously worked right across London from deep in suburbia or beyond — practically all of them — now began and terminated in Central London. The only routes which still connected east and west or north and south were orbital ones, such as the 724 from Harlow to Windsor via St Albans and Uxbridge, the long-established 725 between Dartford, Croydon and Woking (previously Windsor) and its companion 726, which did serve Windsor, the 727, linking Crawley and Luton Airport via Kingston and Watford, the 734 between Addlestone and Hertford via Hounslow and Golders Green and the 750 between Gravesend and Crawley via Bromley. Perhaps even more significant were the airport routes serving Heathrow, Gatwick and Luton. These included all but one of the orbital routes and many of the others. The once frequent and heavily patronised series of routes worked by double-deck RTs and, later, Routemasters from Aldgate, had either disappeared or been changed almost beyond recognition.

GREEN LINE

COACH GUIDE
GOLDEN JUBILEE ISSUE

Summer 1980   Price 20p

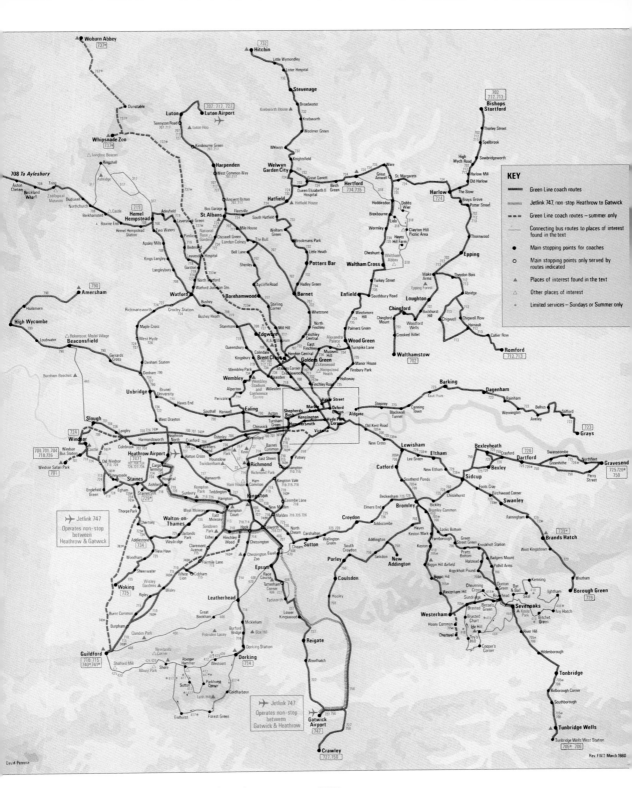

Left and above: Green Line Coach Guide and map, summer 1980.

Above: On 13 July 1980 Green Line's Golden Jubilee was marked by a commemorative run from Golders Green to Crawley. Among approximately 150 vehicles taking part was preserved RW3, a Willowbrook-bodied AEC Reliance of 1960, which, although a bus, was used on Green Line reliefs. It is seen crossing the junction of Kennington Road and Lambeth Road. *Graham Smith*

Right: Also taking part in the run was another preserved bus to have worked Green Line reliefs, this being RT1018, one of the celebrated trio of RTs repainted in NBC leaf green in 1977 and sent to Chelsham garage. *Graham Smith*

London Country in the Early 1980s

The saddest-looking RT of all time? RT1563, minus several vital elements but seemingly still for the main part waterproof, serving as a store at the back of Chelsham garage in March 1981, shortly before being put out of its misery.

BY 1980 the last vestiges of London Transport were fast disappearing from what had been its Country Area. Thirteen Routemasters lasted with London Country just into the decade; all were gone by early March, Chelsham and Swanley being the last garages to operate the type. The final two were both former coaches, RMC1515, fittingly, being used on Chelsham's 403 Express until mid-February, and RMC1512 surviving a few days longer on the 477. Although the latter and RML2446 worked a farewell tour on 1 March, this, as is often the way, was not quite the end, as RMC1512 substituted for a sick Leyland Atlantean on 4/5 March.

Whatever the logistics of two-man operation deep in the rural backwaters of Slough, Dartford, Watford etc, London Transport's affection for the Routemaster was undimmed, and a day after its last working on

the 477 RMC1512 rejoined all its surviving London Country brethren back in the welcoming embrace of 55 Broadway. All, that is, except the Daddy of them all, prototype coach RMC4, which, remarkably for a prototype, had worked in ordinary service, from Hatfield garage, until May 1979 and would be kept as a celebrity. In 1980 it would be seen in a number of starring roles, for this was the year of the Green Line Golden Jubilee. Two of the Routemaster's predecessors, RT1018 and RT1563, were actually still on London Country's books in 1981, the former in NBC leaf green and in use as a trainer, the latter, the saddest-looking RT of all time, battered and minus much of the cab area and engine but still of use, serving as a uniform store at Chelsham. Eventually what was left of RT1563 was broken up, but RT1018 was sold into preservation.

Left: A typical Chelsham scene in February 1980 as an unidentified Marshall-bodied SMW Swift and RMC1515 await their fate. The Swift was soon broken up, but the Routemaster would last somewhat longer, being returned the following month to London Transport, initially for use as a driver trainer, and later returned to limited passenger service as an open-topper.

The Routemasters most desired by London Transport were the London Country RMLs, for these were, to all intents and purposes, identical to their LT brethren. By the late 1970s many were in a deplorable state, lying out of use at various London Country garages. In December 1978 some 38 were bought by London Transport, along with 20 RMCs and 10 RCLs. In March 1979 a further 17 RMLs were sent by LCBS to Yorkshire scrap dealer Wombwell Diesels to be broken up. This clearly took London Transport by surprise and spurred it into action. It quickly bought back all the others and overhauled them. Some needed virtually a complete rebuild, but such was the esteem in which London Transport held the Routemaster, and by May 1981 all the returnees had been painted red and were back in passenger service. Aside from the inherent value of a bus which was now fit for decades' more service, LT was able to avoid the £10,000 per bus it would have had to spend overhauling its unloved DM/DMS Fleetlines, some of which had served but three years. LT's love affair with the Routemaster is yet one more example of how what made sense in the provinces, even in cities as large as Birmingham, Manchester, Sheffield, Leeds and Liverpool, did not necessarily apply in the capital. Half-cab production in the UK had ended in 1969, and by 1980 the one-person operated (OPO) rear-engined double-decker was becoming universal. Yet many of the busiest routes in the heart of the capital were still worked by half-cabs with open rear platforms and conductors and, indeed, would remain so for another 20 years and more.

Below: A coincidence of RCLs on the 149 at Waterloo in March 1981. RCL2256 (left) and RCL2255 (right) were among the 41 one-time Green Line coaches bought back by London Transport and sent to Edmonton and Stamford Hill garages in August 1980. Just about the most comfortable buses ever to run in Central London, internally they retained their various Green Line refinements whilst externally, as can be seen, they kept their original route indicators and their rear lower-deck window arrangement, although the platform doors were removed.

The DMS did not enter service with LT until after the creation of London Country, but in 1980 seven passed into London Country ownership. Although repainted in NBC leaf green they were never employed in passenger service, being restricted to driver-training duties. In the opposite direction, 1980 saw the demise of the ex-Ribble Burlingham-bodied Leyland PD3 trainers, along with the last of the unloved single-deck MB and MBS Merlin classes.

Left: Trainer RCL2245, still in Lincoln green, leads two red RMs towards Hyde Park Corner in the summer of 1980.

Below left: DMS630, one of the seven DMSs sold to London Country for use as driver-trainers, stands on Eccleston Bridge — a venue familiar to generations of Green Line coaches and Country buses — in July 1980. No London Country DMS ever carried passengers, although all seven would return to normal service following sale to Midland Red (East) in 1982/3. *Graham Smith*

Rather more surprising disposals were the standard ECW-bodied Bristol LHSs of the BL class, none having served more than seven years. Also leaving in 1980, for a new life with the Bristol Omnibus Co, were the 15 Bristol VRT/ECW double-deckers of the BT class. Introduced in 1977, they had been intended to work from Chelsham on the 403 but were actually employed north of the river, at Grays. It seems strange that these 15 buses, representing a type that was familiar throughout England and Wales, should have spent but three years in the service of London Country, but their departure is probably explained by the fact that they were non-standard amongst a fleet of Leyland Atlanteans that already numbered more than 200.

Below: Otherwise the National Bus Company's standard double-decker, the Bristol VR did not find favour with London Country, and the 15 bought in 1977 (like BT3 seen at Romford) were sold after only three years. *Ian Allan Library*

In 1981 came the first withdrawals of the narrower (7ft 6in) Bristol LHSs of the BN class, and the departure of the last surviving variations on the disastrous Swift theme, the SMs, SMAs and SMWs. Yet another link with London Transport was broken on 31 December 1981 with the closure of the small garage at East Grinstead garage, which left Crawley as the company's only garage in Sussex. East Grinstead had been home to the eight Daimler

Below: London Country's last buses to derive from London Transport were its longest-serving, the XF class of Daimler Fleetlines based at East Grinstead. XF4 is seen at the Black Horse, Hookwood. *D. Trevor Rowe*

Above: SM454, one of the last Swifts in service with London Country, in St Peter's Street, St Albans, on a misty 26 September 1980. *Graham Smith*

Fleetlines of the XF class, bought by London Transport in 1965 for trial against a batch of Leyland Atlanteans. The Daimlers, which proved marginally more reliable, were the forerunners of LT's troubled DMSs, whilst, somewhat ironically, London Country opted for the Atlantean. With the threat of imminent homelessness looming, the last active Fleetline, XF3, was delicensed on 31 December 1981. London Country did buy a small number of Fleetlines, 11 CRL6-30s with 72-seat Northern Counties bodywork being diverted from Western Welsh in 1972. Classified AF, these were employed down the A22 from East Grinstead at Godstone, where they took over the 410, the latest in a distinguished lineage that included RMLs, RLHs and forward-entrance STLs. Of these only the RMLs had been Chiswick-designed, so it could be argued that the AFs were following traditions (although by this time, of course, all London Country's buses and coaches were being bought 'off the shelf'). The last survivor, AF10, was taken out of service, from Godstone, in October 1982. Curiously, a vastly longer-lived predecessor of the AFs, the former RLH44, which had been converted as a mobile uniform store (581J), departed into preservation in January 1983.

Above: Introduced in 1973, the ECW-bodied Bristol LHSs of the BL class were allocated initially to Dunton Green and St Albans, although many soon gravitated to Amersham. The last of these 8ft-wide vehicles was withdrawn in 1980. *Graham Smith*

Below: Later LHSs were bodied to a reduced width of 7ft 6in. Highest-numbered BN67, delivered in 1977, is seen some 10 years later adorned with 'Chilternlink' MAP insignia. *Graham Smith*

The AEC Reliance had, in its early days, been scarcely more reliable (there's a pun there somewhere) than the Merlins and Swifts. In 1971/2 London Country had bought 90 with 45-seat Park Royal bodies — the RP class —for Green Line service. Their careers on such work were brief, although the Leyland Nationals which followed were scarcely any better; more reliable they may have been, but in terms of passenger appeal they were entirely unsuited to Green Line work (the early examples, in particular, being no more than less-well-appointed buses) and were soon demoted. By 1980 the RPs too were regarded as buses, although, like the Nationals, they continued to pop up as substitutes on Green Line duties. With the withdawal of the last, RP25, in February 1984, there remained in London Country service just one group of AECs — the 150 Reliances of the RS and RB classes, bodied respectively by Plaxton (in **S**carborough) and Duple (in **B**lackpool). Delivered in the years 1977-9, by which time the Reliance had been cured of its faults, these brought a new, upmarket image to the Green Line network, their genuine coach bodywork being virtually identical to that found across the road from the Eccleston Bridge Green Line stops, at Victoria Coach Station.

Above: New in 1972 as a Green Line coach, Park Royal-bodied AEC Reliance RP20 works a local bus service in St Albans on 26 September 1980. The last of these unreliable vehicles would be taken out of service in 1985. *Graham Smith*

Below: RP2 of Reigate, decked out in leaf green and white but with evidence of ownership, other than the NBC double arrow, all but faded away, finds itself passing the Railway Hotel, Reigate, while on rail-replacement duty. *Graham Smith*

Above: RB135, a Duple-bodied AEC Reliance coach decked out in Green Line Golden Jubilee livery, at Bournemouth in the summer of 1980, having arrived on a National Express working from London.

Below: Jubilee-liveried AEC Reliance/Plaxton RS137, sporting 'Green Line 50' logo, heads down Park Lane on route 717, 19 June 1980. *Graham Smith*

Above: Between 1972 and 1981 London Country took 293 Leyland Atlanteans; all formed the AN class, bodied by Park Royal, MCW or Roe. AN141 was allocated to Crawley for the town's 'C-Line' network. *David Stuttard*

Below: At Stevenage, on the northern tip of London Country's Polo-shaped operating area, routes were branded 'Stevenage Bus'. AN158 demonstrates. *Ian Allan Library*

Although early examples were decked out and used as Green Line coaches, the Leyland National was ill suited for such work. Despite being officially relieved of these duties by the 1980s, the type continued to be substituted throughout the decade. London Country (South West) SNB423 is seen blinded for the 716 route in June 1989.

Whilst no-one could really pretend that the Leyland National, in whatever fancy livery you chose to paint it, was anything but a workaday bus, it was in some respects a success (although just how much of a success will forever be debated). London Country loved it and by 1980 owned no fewer than 540, the largest fleet of Nationals in the world; London Transport, at this stage, had around 430.

Equally popular with London Country was the Leyland Atlantean double-decker, which, like the AEC Reliance, had developed into a reliable breed. The first examples of the AN class had replaced RTs in 1972, and the type was still being delivered in the early 1980s. Fitted with either Park Royal or almost-identical Roe bodywork, they were amongst the most handsome of all rear-engined double-deckers of the 1970s and '80s. The last new ANs were delivered early in 1981, by which time the class numbered nearly 300, but this was not the end, for second-hand examples would later join the fleet.

With every year that air travel increased, conveying passengers to and from Heathrow (the busiest airport in the world), Gatwick (not all that far behind), Luton and Stansted became more lucrative. In many ways the coach was ideally suited for air travellers, for whilst Heathrow was served by Underground — the Piccadilly Line — and Gatwick by main-line trains from Victoria, London Bridge and the South Coast, the others had no direct rail links; and, in any case, the coach services were aimed principally at the holidaymaker rather than the business traveller, who was often accustomed to coach travel and did not want the ever-growing hassle of driving to the airport and finding parking, to say nothing of the rip-off which has always been a feature of airport parking charges. January 1980 saw the launch of Flightline 767 between Victoria Coach Station and Heathrow,

coaches being provided by Green Line and Alder Valley. The fare was £1.50, which compared favourably with LT's Airbus (worked by double-deck MCW Metrobuses) at £2, an Underground fare of £2.20 and a whole lot more if you were rash enough to hail a taxi. The *London Bus Magazine* commented that 'It is expected to prove especially popular with the growing numbers of travellers using the low-cost National Express coach network … connecting under one roof at Victoria Coach Station.' Luton Airport, at a cost of £2 for a single fare, was served by Flightline 757; this, with an 'approximate journey time of 70min … by luxury coach … will set you down right beside Victoria Coach Station, which is the only terminal in London to offer connections to all parts of the country'.

In 1980 long-distance coach services were deregulated, and the Green Line network expanded, a situation to some extent mirroring that of the late 1920s and early 1930s, when there was something of a free-for-all, although there was also a good deal of co-operation with other NBC operators. Among a number of innovations were weekend Seaside Specials, the 709, for example, being extended way beyond Forest Row to Sheffield Park, for the Bluebell

Above: The livery adopted initially for the Flightline 777 service between Victoria and Gatwick Airport was an adaptation of that devised for Green Line's Golden Jubilee. Reliance/Plaxton RS136 demonstrates in June 1981, the dual fleetname additionally revealing that the service was worked jointly with Southdown. *Graham Smith*

Above: From time to time examples of the large AN class of Leyland Atlanteans turned out on Green Line work, like AN259 seen with wrap-around advertisement for the 'Happy Eater' restaurant chain. *G. W. Girling*

Below: London Country's Leyland Olympians made their debut on former London Transport route 84, taken over on 24 April 1982. A year later LR3 passes The White Hart in South Mimms on its way north. *Kevin Lane*

Above: Towards the future. Serving the numerous airports within its territory became an ever more lucrative aspect of London Country's business, and the company was not slow to advertise the fact with all manner of livery variations. An almost new green, white and yellow Leyland Tiger/Duple, TD37, and a pretty pink, pale-blue and white prospective passenger meet at Gatwick Airport in the summer of 1983.

Railway, and on to Brighton. Then there was the 768, which ran between Kingston and Brighton and, like the 709, proved sufficiently popular for double-deck Leylands, both Atlanteans and Olympians (which latter would join the fleet from 1982) to be employed quite regularly. Green Line coaches — proper ones — now appeared regularly at Oxford and Cambridge, the latter being served by the 797/798, operated jointly with Eastern Counties. Another joint service, this time with United Counties, was the 760 between Heathrow and Northampton, whilst Southdown contributed to Flightline 777, between Victoria, Gatwick Airport and Crawley.

Yet another joint service (and one which like so many, would be short-lived) was the 795, inaugurated on 1 April 1983 between Southend and Brighton, was extraordinary in that it involved not only three NBC subsidiaries — Green Line, Eastern National and Southdown — but also Southend Transport. Possibly its chief value was the link it provided between Essex and Gatwick Airport. A close relation (and the sole concern of Green Line) was the 796, which ran between Stevenage and Brighton via Romford.

Introduced later that year between Hemel Hempstead and Waltham Cross was the 'Speedline' 750, expected to be 'particularly useful for shoppers, students, hospital staff and visitors, and airline passengers'. Sadly all of them preferred their cars. Nevertheless all this enterprise paid off, for in the years 1981-3 Green Line helped London Country return a small profit, although that made from private-hire, contract and National Express work was much greater. The National Express involvement meant that the Green Line brand was seen far and wide, whilst National Express coaches often appeared on traditional Green Line services.

Above: Green Line TP11, a Plaxton-bodied Leyland Tiger delivered early in 1984 to Hertford garage, is seen in 1985 parked at Tolpuddle, the Dorset village where, every year, a great parade is held to mark the beginning of the trade-union movement. The principal speaker that year was Neil Kinnock, leader of the Labour Party.

Below: Long before the creation of London Transport in 1933 London-based bus companies had operated routes far beyond London and what became the LPTB Country Area. Now, in the 1980s, London Country extended its Green Line network back into some of those areas. One of twenty 12m Duple-bodied Leyland Tigers delivered in the spring of 1986, TDL53 gazes out to sea from Brighton's Pool Valley bus station in the summer of 1988.

Left: Oxford became another regular Green Line destination. TP68, a Plaxton-bodied Leyland Tiger of 1985, waits in the city's Gloucester Green coach station in the summer of 1989.

Above: Arguably the most impressive vehicles used on Green Line work in the 1980s were 15 long-wheelbase Leyland Olympian/ECW 72-seater coaches, of which the first five arrived in 1984. Similar to vehicles used on commuter services by Maidstone & District and Alder Valley, these were allocated to Northfleet, whence they chiefly worked the 720 between Gravesend and Victoria. However, as revealed by this view of LRC4 in the Strand in April 1985, they sometimes strayed to other duties.

• 4 •

Underground Downs and Ups

FOLLOWING the creation of London Regional Transport in June 1984, London Underground Ltd (LUL) was set up in 1985 as a wholly owned subsidiary. Nicholas Ridley, Margaret Thatcher's Secretary of State for Transport, declared on 29 June 1984 in a speech in the House of Commons during the passing of the London Regional Transport Act which took control away from the Great London Council, 'I have returned the running of buses and tubes to professional managers'.

In reality, despite Ridley's declared philosophy, Government still had a good deal to say about how the Underground should be run, and LUL was required, amongst other things, to ensure that 'real fares be held broadly stable beyond January 1985' and that 'the needs of disabled people be given special attention', as well as providing 'improved interchanges and travelling environments'. What was needed to ensure that the Underground worked most effectively was, of course (as history had long taught in such situations), a mixture of private enterprise and state overview — as would eventually be achieved.

Fortunately the professional managers were well qualified to do their job and, after decades of decline (since 1949, in fact), travel on the Underground began to increase sharply in the 1980s. In 1982, following the disastrous end to the 'Fares Fair' scheme — and a 96% hike in fares — in March, there were fewer than 500 million journeys made, the lowest number since 1943. However, a bright dawn was just over the horizon. The GLC, in one if its last acts before abolition, managed to reduce fares by 25%, and this, with the introduction of the London Travelcard scheme, with its six zones, and changing social habits, with more and more people travelling off-peak, contributed to an increase to 563 million journeys in 1983 and 659 million in 1984 — a trend which would continue throughout the decade and beyond.

Some parts of the Underground system, usually outlying Home Counties branches, were always likely to become casualties when times got bad. One such was the Central Line's Epping–Ongar branch in rural Essex. Single-track and worked by a single train, it carried fewer than 1,000 passengers daily, although it has to be said that there were plenty of stations on the British Rail network which would have been happy to have approached this figure. Closure was proposed but refused, although the little-used Blake Hall station, which Essex County Council refused to subsidise, closed on 31 October 1981. However, trains were reduced to rush-hours only. The line would eventually close completely in 1994, although a preservation group was established in the hope of reviving it in some form or another.

One of the curiosities of the system — albeit not the only one — was the sharing, by the Bakerloo Line, of tracks with the London Midland Region of British Rail from Willesden Junction to Watford Junction, a situation which dated back to London & North Western days and World War 1. Tube trains ceased running beyond Stonebridge Park on 24 September 1982, but a deep longing for the sylvan shades of outer suburbia saw services restored as far as Harrow & Wealdstone on a bright summer's morning in June two years later.

On the positive side, the 1980s saw the introduction of a new type of surface stock, known as 'D78'. Delivered in the summer of 1979, the first of these three-car units entered regular passenger service on the District Line on 28 January 1980. Similar in appearance to the 'C' stock but with bodyshells constructed entirely of aluminium, the 75 trains were built in Birmingham by Metro-Cammell. Each car was around 60ft long, such that a six-car formation was able to replace a seven-car train of shorter vehicles with no reduction in capacity, and had four doors, which, contrasting with previous practice, were single-leaf sliding items, 3ft 6in wide.

Above: Trains of District Line 'CO'/'CP' stock stabled in the sidings at Ealing Broadway on a gloomy December day in 1979. The track workers in the foreground are attending to the Western Region main line.

Below: Upminster depot in March 1980, with 'CO'/'CP' District Line stock in red or unpainted aluminium.

Above: Trains of 1938 Tube stock and 'CO'/'CP' surface stock on display at Acton Works, 3 July 1983. *John Glover*

Left: A train of 1938 stock eases out of the turnback siding at Harrow & Wealdstone and draws into the platform to take up passenger duty in July 1984. In its day this large fleet operated the whole of the Northern Line, including the Northern City, both branches of the Bakerloo (with an additional pre-1938 trailer) and some Piccadilly Line services. *John Glover*

Above: The Hammersmith & City service is operated by trains of 'C' stock, the four sets of doors on each side of the car making these units very effective in shifting crowds. This is an eastbound service, approaching Ladbroke Grove in August 1989. *John Glover*

Below: A 'C'-stock train arrives at Parsons Green on a District Line service for Edgware Road in September 1985. The 'D' stock in the sidings on right is rather improbably standing on brick arches, these being all that remains of the long-abandoned quadrupling scheme. *John Glover*

Above: Earl's Court in March 1989. As darkness approaches, a train of 'D' stock train bound for Plaistow stands at the platform. The red panel on the front of these trains, which were delivered between 1979 and 1983, was one of the few variations from an all-over aluminium finish in this period. *John Glover*

Below: Surrey Docks, September 1985. For a short while the East London line was operated by three-car sets of 'D' stock, represented by this train emerging into sunshine on its way to New Cross Gate. They were later replaced by 'A' stock, which served until closure of the line in December 2007. In 2011 it will be reopened as part of London Overground's through route to East Croydon. *John Glover*

Left: The branch to Kensington Olympia diverges from the main District Line at West Kensington East Junction. When this photograph was taken, in July 1989, the shuttle service from High Street Kensington was being operated by a train of 'D' stock. *John Glover*

The interior layout was influenced by research which had shown that having most of the seating arranged along the sides, with plenty of space for circulation around the doors, was the optimum for high-density Underground trains operating at times of peak occupancy, when most passengers travelled short distances and were prepared to stand, hanging on to the plentiful grab-rails provided.

In another innovation, the 'D78' stock allowed passengers to operate doors. This had been tried, without much success, in the 1950s and '60s, but now the travelling public took to the notion, it was claimed, and it was gradually adopted throughout the network. The driver had over-riding control of door opening and closing which meant OPO was now feasible, and, with radio communication with the line controller, cameras, screens and mirrors at each station, the Circle Line duly became OPO in 1984, the District Line following suit a year later.

The first 20 'D78' units were double-cabbed, with automatic couplers at each driving end; the remainder comprised 65 east- and 65 west-facing single-cab, three-car units, the last arriving in June 1983. Technically similar to the 1973 Tube stock, with Tube-sized wheels, these new trains brought to a close the careers of the celebrated 'CO'/'CP' stock of the immediate prewar years and the very similar looking 'R' stock, the last of which had not entered service until 1959 and was thus hardly ancient by Underground standards. It was decided that all would be withdrawn in order that the District Line could be worked by uniformly modern stock. The last 'CP' trains — two six-car units — ended work after a series of special runs on 31 March 1981 and were the last all-red surface trains. Two years later almost to the day, on 5 March 1983, the 'R' stock ceased work.

• 5 •

Jubilee No 2:
London Transport

ONE of the great jazz standards is 'Jubilee', especially when sung by Louis Armstrong. Whilst the London Transport empire has never yet stretched to New Orleans, the Jubilee of 1983 was very much a celebration, a joyful event commemorating 50 pretty glorious years, and if you were lucky enough to ride the skid pad in an RT at Chiswick during the Golden Jubilee Gala, staged on the weekend on 2/3 July (as my three boys and I did), then you certainly swung.

But before we look at the gala itself we would do well to consider the context in which it was held, as outlined in the introduction to the souvenir guide. In looking back at the problems — chiefly falling passenger numbers and increasing traffic congestion — faced since the 1950s, this noted that ' "Bus-only" lanes, first introduced in 1968, helped London Transport to combat traffic congestion, but the most significant change of the late 1960s was the progressive introduction of one-man-operated buses, which allowed considerable savings on staff costs.' So it did, but it was not a progressive move. My Uncle Harry, who, as a City executive and a churchwarden, could hardly be considered anything other than a pillar of the establishment (but used to vote Labour, partly — the rest of the family used to think — to irritate his wife, Aunt Dorothy, whom he loved dearly but who, he considered, rather too enthusiastically embraced the semi-detached 'Tudorbethan' outer-suburban lifestyle his income allowed), once told me he considered the police force 'a necessary evil'. So it was with one-man operation. It may have been necessary, but delays increased, and the absence of a conductor encouraged vandalism and did nothing to reassure passengers.

The introduction continues: 'Various teething troubles were experienced, particularly with the first generation of front-entrance, rear-engined vehicles acquired for one-man operation [the single-deck Merlins and Swifts and double-deck DMSs] and the cumbersome automatic fare-collection equipment which delayed boarding times. Unlike most earlier bus types, the new vehicles were not designed by London Transport's own engineering staff, and they did not cope well with London's gruelling stop-start traffic conditions.' Again, not the whole picture, for there was also a failure throughout London Transport to recognise that the problems were far greater than engineering malfunctions; the DMSs for example, many of which were still at work in 1983 (but rapidly being disposed of), performed perfectly well with their new owners on the streets of Birmingham, Manchester and Glasgow, where 'gruelling stop-start traffic conditions' were not unknown. The introduction adds that 'many of them have now been replaced by a second generation of far more reliable front-entrance buses supplied since the late 1970s by Leyland and Metro-Cammell Weymann.' These were the T-class Titans, which certainly had a great deal of LT input, and the M-class Metrobuses, which had a lot less but still performed quite adequately.

Reading on, we learn that 'the central and continuing issue of concern to London Transport in the 1980s is finance. Whether it is a matter of fare levels subsidy or capital investment, the crucial questions are always: "How much will it cost?" and "Who is going to pay for it?" … London Transport will need the support of the planners and politicians, those who have the power to approve and finance the important new transportation projects which London so badly needs. With their backing, London Transport can make the next 50 years as memorable as the first.' Long before we got even halfway there — which is where we are now — London Transport would cease to exist, being replaced by Transport for London, although as far as the average passenger was concerned, this meant little more than did the London Passenger Transport Board becoming the London Transport Executive in 1948. Certainly finance (and who provides it), along with planners and politicians, would have as big a role to play, as always. What is not mentioned is ownership, and in that aspect of the London bus, train and tram scene

we are back, in a sense, to where we were before 1933. Note also the inclusion of 'tram'. The souvenir guide highlights 'two important new schemes which have already been given the go-ahead'. One was the Piccadilly Line extension to Heathrow Terminal 4, the other 'light-rail transit system to link Docklands with the City … involving running modern single-deck trams'. In the event the vehicles working this are generally regarded as trains rather than trams, although the still-expanding system is certainly 'light rail', but the following decade would see the return to London of what undoubtedly *were* trams, the first Tramlink cars appearing on the streets of Croydon in 1999.

The Golden Jubilee Gala encompassed both the Acton and Chiswick Works. London Transport had always been good at commemorations and preservation, and by 1983 so were a lot of other people — transport operators, societies and individuals. The London Omnibus Traction Society (LOTS) had been around since 1964, providing an invaluable service, chiefly to enthusiasts but also to operators, who were sometimes one and the same, faithfully recording the public transport scene month by month. The London Bus Preservation Trust had held its first open day at its Cobham headquarters

Pioneer DMS1 had by now joined the ranks of the officially preserved and had been sent off to join the Science Museum collection at its outstation high on the downs above Swindon at the former Wroughton Aerodrome, where it is seen at an open day. A number of London vehicles were to be found here, the 'Q1' trolleybus, for instance, being stored, somewhat incongruously, alongside two prewar airliners.

in 1974, its ever-expanding collection of vintage vehicles not merely complementing the official LT collection but also providing many individuals with the incentive to enter the preservation field themselves. Thus 1983 saw many events celebrating London Transport's Golden Jubilee, ranging from the one-off appearance of a preserved RT to large rallies. But the Gala held at Chiswick and Acton was special, not least because it was something of a swansong, an event that could never be repeated. Later that year, after a similar event staged at Aldenham Works, it was announced that this latter was to close and that the future of Chiswick was under consideration. By the end of the decade it was gone, sold off to Bus Engineering Ltd, under which auspices it was to survive for a brief while before being razed to the ground.

The official London Transport Collection had led a somewhat peripatetic existence since first being displayed to the public in 1963 at the former Clapham bus garage. Having moved from there to Syon Park, it finally settled in the heart of London, at Covent Garden. Back in the 1960s I had worked at a florist's in Wimbledon, collecting flowers before dawn from Covent Garden market. This was a highly atmospheric location, not least on account of the cafés and pubs catering for the colourful characters who worked there, but in the 1970s the flower market moved to Nine Elms, and the wonderful iron-and-glass building designed by William Rogers and built in 1871/2 by William Cubitt & Co (a firm much involved in the 19th-century heyday of railway construction) was threatened with destruction. Eventually, after a long campaign, the complex was saved, and the erstwhile flower market became home to the London Transport Museum, which first opened its doors to the public on 29 March 1980. Various adaptations had been necessary, notably the installation of a strong platform to carry rail vehicles, and the building was not large enough to house anything like the complete collection, but its central position, beside what rapidly became one of the most popular retail outlets and tourist attractions in the capital, more than compensated for this.

But back to Chiswick. On that bright July morning in 1983 it would have been inconceivable that the complex, highly organised engineering headquarters of the world's greatest urban transport organisation

Above left: In 1980 the official London Transport Collection moved to Covent Garden, where the new London Transport Museum opened to the public on 29 March 1980. 'Feltham' tram No 355 is seen shortly afterwards restored to its original (1931) MET livery.

Left: A line-up of London buses at the newly opened London Transport Museum, featuring the highest-numbered RT, RT4825, next to 'sit-up-and-beg' STL469, LT165, ST821, and NS1995.

Above: The opening of the London Transport Museum was followed by a revival of vintage bus route 100 through Central London. Here ex-Thomas Tilling ST922, rescued for preservation by Prince Marshall, stands outside the handsome museum buildings in Covent Garden.

Below: Another, even older participant on route 100 was D142, a three-ton Dennis with Dodson body, new in 1925 to 'London Public' and nowadays based at Cobham Bus Museum. It is seen from the upper-deck of a Routemaster heading past Charing Cross station in May 1981.

(which, as we enthusiasts knew who were first bitten by the bug in the 1940s, had been there for ever), could completely disappear. My boys and I took ourselves off to Wareham station, and, removing the Dorset straw from behind our ears and practising our West London drawl, boarded the 08.35 for Waterloo, thence the District Line to Gunnersbury, and presented ourselves at the gates of Mecca. Thus I had regarded Chiswick Works ever since 1947, when Clive Gillam had informed me of its existence. I'd several times stood at its gates, but, unlike most engine sheds, this was not somewhere one could infiltrate unseen by the armed sentinels. But there would be no such thwarting for my boys; we were going straight in, not sneakily but by invitation — well, once we had paid our entrance fee. The highlight was the ride on the skid bus. The Skid Bus Experience was provided by three vehicles — two RTs and an RMC. The RT class had bowed out of public service in 1979, but several examples were retained for various purposes. By 1983 there were just four left. RT2958 was a radio training vehicle, and RT3065 was beyond resuscitation, so it was RT1530 and RT2143 which were the very last to carry passengers whilst still in LT ownership, giving us a thrill as we gracefully glided over the Chiswick skidpan.

At least, I *think* that was the highlight, although honesty compels me to admit that for the boys this may have been an invitation to sit astride a Police motor cycle. There was also a demonstration of how to right a double-deck bus after it had toppled over — not, I hasten to add, on the skidpan, which always looked a lot more dangerous than it really was. Other attractions included model road and rail layouts, a full-size bus you could drive (but not if you were under 10, 'Bertie' the playbus being provided for this age group) and refreshments in the LT canteen (the only such establishment normally open to the public being that in Harrow bus station) and a vast array of stalls manned by enthusiast groups. There was also a display of ancillary vehicles, one which particularly caught my eye being a splendid Albion tanker dating from 1938, ELP 615, which, although it seems never to have belonged to London Transport, might well have done, for both STLs and 10T10s had registrations in the ELP series.

Last but by no means least was the bus rally, featuring not only London buses, past and present, but also their provincial cousins. The latter were mainly AECs — naturally enough, given that the Southall manufacturer had for generations been the principal supplier of London buses and that its factory had been just down the road from Chiswick. There were prewar Regents from Provincial and Brighton, the latter (FUF 63), one of the truly handsome Weymann-bodied Regents of 1939, posed, intriguingly, alongside the almost identical STL2692, dating from 1945, restored to its original Country Area livery. Then there were a number of Routemasters, beautifully maintained with various extra embellishments and liveries, the pride of their respective garages, including at least three most fetchingly repainted in the 1933 livery of red and white with black lining and silver roof, looking as though it had been designed specifically with the

Above right: Looking a good deal more distinguished than its standard brethren, Leyland National LS402, in LT Golden Jubilee livery, heads for South Harrow station in June 1983.
Graham Smith

Right: Possibly the most popular attraction at the 2 July 1983 Golden Jubilee celebration at Chiswick was a ride on the skid bus. Becoming the last RT to carry passengers whilst still in London Transport ownership, RT1530 is seen performing for an appreciative audience. Note the interesting array of vehicles in the background.

Routemaster in mind; although to be fair DMS1933 also wore a version of this livery and looked equally splendid. RM1983 was adorned in gold, to commemorate the Jubilee, a forerunner of those that would celebrate HM Queen Elizabeth's Golden Jubilee in 2002. One began to realise that a Routemaster didn't have to be red all over and that all sorts of imaginative liveries, as long as they took into account the lines of the bus, could do wonders for its appearance.

Finally there was a line-up of what purported to be the first eight Routemasters, although there is evidence to suggest that 'RM5' was really RM555, the real RM5 being under repair at Palmers Green garage. To quote S. P. Newman in the *London Bus Magazine*, 'It is not for me to comment on why ... LT wishes to operate in such mysterious ways.' Nor me. But it certainly looked good. Decades later, after popping into the Chinese Embassy — more or less opposite Broadcasting House — for a visa, I found myself boarding RM5 on route 38. It carried a plaque noting that it was the lowest-numbered production Routemaster. The conductress and I (now that lady actors can no longer be called actresses is it politically correct to refer to conductresses, even if they possess shapely legs and other feminine attributes?) got into conversation, and she asked me where RM1-4 were. 'Popping in for a Chinese visa' and 'boarding RM5' are not phrases one would have envisaged sitting easily side by side when Routemasters first entered regular service back in June 1959. Nor, for that matter, might one have expected to ride through the depths of the Buckinghamshire countryside in a gold-liveried RM5 more than 40 years later.

Above: Some of the buses on display at Chiswick on 2 July 1983, with Airbus Metrobus M434 showing off its much neater rear end compared with that of gold-liveried Titan T747.

Above right: Two examples of just how splendid a Routemaster could look when adorned in non-standard livery. RM2116, from Seven Kings garage, wears an adaptation of the 1933 London Transport livery, which was more or less identical to that of the LGOC, whilst no explanation is needed for the gold livery of Sidcup's RM1983.

Right: A line-up at Chiswick of the (alleged) first eight Routemasters, with the four prototypes prominent.

• 6 •

Some Good Things Come to an End

IN THE pantheon of distinguished Leyland models, the Titan was right up there, having been the Lancashire manufacturer's standard double-decker from 1927 until the end of half-cab production in 1969, but London Transport was linked inextricably with AEC. It had, however, inherited a number of Titan TD1s and TD2s in 1933, bought 100 TD4s in 1937, acquired some far less popular 'unfrozen' TD7s during World War 2 and bought 65 PD1s immediately afterwards, plus of course the 500 RTWs and 1,631 RTLs of the postwar era.

Whether it was wise to revive the Titan name in 1977 for a rear-engined bus is debatable; given the far-from-spotless reputation of Leyland buses of the period, the company was certainly taking a risk. The bus in question, identified originally as Project B15 and unveiled to the press two years earlier, was Leyland's great hope for the future, an integral-construction vehicle intended to replace not only the Atlantean but also the Daimler (now Leyland) Fleetline and Bristol VRT. London Transport was consulted at every stage of its development, and the

intention was that the Titan should be built in London, initially by Park Royal, before transfer of production to the AEC works at Southall. Although London Transport was keen to take the type in significant numbers, the GLC authorising an initial order for 250, to be followed by a similar number in 1980/1, by 1979 productivity was so poor that closure of both factories was announced. There had been a possibility of moving Titan production to the ECW works at Lowestoft, but this came to nought, and in the summer of 1980, LT's first batch of 250 having been completed at Park Royal, jigs, parts and equipment were moved to the Leyland National plant at Workington, Cumbria, where

Left: An almost deserted Trafalgar Square in June 1980 sees Titan T81 shortly after dawn at the terminus of night bus N98.

Above: With the famous tea clipper *Cutty Sark* in the background, where else could this be but Greenwich? Titan T832 prepares to head for the heights of Upper Norwood as another of the class waits for the traffic to clear in the summer of 1982.

production resumed the following year. Thereafter the type featured largely in London Transport's orders, such that by the end of 1984 some 1,125 had been delivered.

Rivalling the Titan for LT's affections in the early 1980s was the MCW Metrobus. This had its origins in the Metropolitan, a joint venture of the 1970s between MCW and Swedish manufacturer Scania that had attracted an order from LT for 164 buses (the MD class). Encouraged by its success, MCW decided to go it alone, designing an integral-construction vehicle and fitting it with the well-tried and popular Gardner engine. LT followed a trial batch of five with an order for 200 followed by another for a further 200 which was subsequently increased to 300 to compensate for the delays with Titan deliveries. The type soon became a familiar sight in West London (the former tram/trolleybus depot at Fulwell being a notable early recipient) and later expanded its sphere of operations northwards and eastwards. Notable among the earlier deliveries were M431-46, which in November 1980 inaugurated 'Airbus' routes A1 and A2 between Victoria/Paddington respectively and Heathrow; on these vehicles a large luggage area was

created downstairs by fitting only nine seats (rather than 28), plus the usual 43 upstairs. In 1984 the original Airbus fleet (itself bolstered by later conversions) was replaced by M1006-29, fitted with coach-type seats, luggage lockers and carpets upstairs. By this time air traffic was expanding at a phenomenal rate, all but doubling between 1980 and 1990, and Heathrow had become a fair-sized town with numerous routes, not only those of London Transport, National Express and others connecting with the outside world but also various internal services serving car parks and staff; long-gone were the days when redundant 30-seat TDs could be used to ferry passengers to or from Lockheed Constellations, Douglas Skymasters and 28-berth Boeing Stratocruisers and BEA's RF-type one-and-a-half-deckers would display the destination of the next departure!

A neat-looking bus, bearing a clear family resemblance to the DMS and the Metropolitan (and perpetuating the latter's asymmetrical windscreen),

the Metrobus sold well in the provinces, although London Transport was its biggest customer. Not generally regarded as being as well proportioned, with its lower-deck windows deeper than those on the upper deck and its far-from-pretty rear aspect, the Titan was nevertheless a distinctive vehicle. Just as the Metrobus could be found mostly to the west of a line down the Hertford Road and the Brighton Road, so the Titan's native hearth — initially, at least — was to the east of this.

Above: Delivered the previous year, Metrobus M445 leaves little doubt as to the service is working as it eases its way through Knightsbridge traffic on its way to Heathrow Airport in May 1981.

Right: LT's Airbus routes replaced the previous British Airways service between Central London and Heathrow. Seen at Victoria are a pair of Roe-bodied Leyland Atlanteans that had been new to BOAC almost a decade earlier.

Metrobus M697 at Brimsdown, November 1986.
Michael M. Collins

Between them the Metrobus and the Titan would dominate the double-deck scene in London throughout the 1980s. By 1983, however, London Transport found itself back in the position of buying what were essentially bespoke buses, for few other operators had taken any real interest in the Titan following its early production problems, while the original version of the Metrobus had elsewhere been superseded by a simplified Mk2 version which employed fewer parts and was therefore cheaper to produce. Thus LT embarked upon a trial — grandly entitled the Alternative Vehicle Evaluation — of new chassis types.

Leyland had addressed operators' reluctance to purchase the integral Titan by developing the simpler Olympian, which was supplied as a conventional chassis and thus allowed customers to specify their

Left: M1191, one of the float Metrobuses each summer converted temporarily for Airbus work and based at Stamford Brook garage, at Heathrow on 31 July 1985. *Graham Smith*

own choice of bodywork. Developed as the B45, it first appeared as the Olympian at the 1980 Commercial Motor Show and went on to fulfil the role that had been expected of the Titan in replacing the Fleetline, the VR and ultimately the Atlantean in Leyland's model range. It was thus an obvious choice for LT to consider, and three, with ECW bodywork, were ordered late in 1983. Arriving early in 1984, they were tried against three Dennis Dominators (built in Guildford) with Northern Counties bodywork, a trio of Alexander-bodied Volvo Ailsas (all the way from Scotland but with strong Viking connections) and a pair of Mk 2 Metrobuses. Of these last, M1441 was not mechanically very different (and looked much the same save for the absence of the original model's trademark asymmetrical windscreen), whereas M1442 had a Cummins L10 engine and a Maxwell gearbox. A third Metrobus, which was expected to be effectively a prototype Mk 3 version, never materialised.

Top: Of the vehicles ordered for the AVE trials, the three L-class Leyland Olympians with ECW bodywork arrived first, going into service on the 170 at the end of March 1984. Its features clearly derived from the Titan, L3 is in Putney Heath that August. *Tony Wilson*

Right: The Volvo Citybus represented opportunities eventually wasted by LBL - with a front engine, it could have had a rear door, and one (V3) did! In August 1984 V2 is seen at Nine Elms. *Tony Wilson*

Below right: M1441/2, the latter of which is crossing Westminster Bridge in April 1985, were the MkII variety of MCW Metrobuses, with a more simplified look to them. *Tony Wilson*

Above: Three Northern Counties-bodied Dennis Dominators completed the AVE trials, and represented a chassis/body combination not used in London since wartime. Short working to Vauxhall, H3 leaves a snowy Roehampton on 13 February 1985, nine days into service. *Tony Wilson*

Left: Although events invalidated the AVE trials, technological innovation continued. An underfloor-engined Volvo Citybus with a hydrostatic system of transmission that conserved power while braking, C1 was used intermittently on Palmers Green's route 102 over 1986/7. It is seen at the route's Golders Green stand in July 1986. *Tony Wilson*

Above: Almost new Leyland Olympian L180 at the entrance to its home, Norwood garage. London's 1986/7 batch of 260 Olympians were amongst the last buses to be bodied by ECW.

Below: Two East Lancs-bodied Leyland Olympian coaches formed the LC class and were assigned to the Eastbourne run of the ultimately short-lived London Liner concept. On 21 August 1986 LC2 is seen opposite Bromley garage. *R. J. Waterhouse*

It was the Olympian that came out on top, and London Transport duly ordered 260 (not a lot by LT standards), with Gardner 6LXB engines and Voith D851 gearboxes. Delivered between January 1986 and January 1987 and allocated to garages in South and South East London, they were amongst the last buses to be bodied by Eastern Coach Works; indeed, L263 was the very last vehicle to be completed at the famous 'Coach Factory' in Lowestoft.

In the meantime deliveries of new Mk1 Metrobuses had been completed in January 1986 with the arrival of M1440, but the following year their numbers were bolstered by five acquired *second-hand* from Greater Manchester, while from West Yorkshire came a pair of Mk2s and, even more unusually, two with Alexander bodywork. Other people's rejects were fast becoming accepted by London Country, but it was a bit of a shock to find London Transport following this path. By this time new vehicles also were being ordered on a piecemeal basis to meet specific needs, and the winter of 1987/8 saw 29 Mk2s placed in service in the Harrow area. These again looked different, being finished in Harrow Buses' attractive livery of red and off-white and being to single- rather than dual-door layout, as was the London standard. Finally a further five second-hand examples, this time from Busways (formerly Tyne & Wear), arrived in 1988, taking the class total to 1,485.

Another 28 Leyland Olympians, bodied by Northern Counties, entered service with Bexleybus (of which more anon) in January 1988, while a further 23 — Cummins-engined examples with Leyland's own bodywork to the earlier ECW design — arrived at the very end of the decade, in December 1989. Perhaps more noteworthy, however, were a pair bodied by East Lancs — another supplier new to London — and delivered in the summer of 1986 for a service, branded 'London Liner' and operated jointly with Eastbourne Buses (which employed similar vehicles), between the capital and the East Sussex resort.

A somewhat belated product of the Transport Act 1980, the 'London Liner' concept had been pioneered in March 1986 in a similar joint venture with the West Midlands Passenger Transport Executive, this being a daily service running at two-hourly intervals between London and Birmingham. The journey took a creditable 2½ hours — 2 hours being the best train time in steam days — and stewards, refreshments and toilets were a feature of each coach. Initially single-deckers were used, London's initial contribution being a trio of Duple-bodied DAFs (another make unthinkable in London just a few years earlier), but these were soon replaced by four double-deck MCW Metroliners. Arguably the most visually impressive vehicle design ever operated by LT/LBL, the Metroliner had its origins in none other than our old friend the Metrobus, though these imposing six-wheelers bore little resemblance to the type that could now be found throughout North and West London.

Sadly intense competition saw London Buses withdraw from both 'London Liner' services before the decade was out. As a result the Olympians and Metroliners used thereon had short lives in London ownership, but their more humble ancestors would continue to provide good service in the capital for years to come, many surviving well into the 21st century.

About to return to the capital on the 'London Liner' service, MCW Metroliner ML2 is passed by a Mk2 Metrobus of West Midlands PTE in Birmingham in May 1986. *Adrian Pearson*

• 7 •

Varying Fortunes — The Routemaster and the DMS

THE service cuts of September 1982, following the House of Lords ruling against the GLC, resulted in the first large-scale withdrawal of Routemasters by London Transport. Some 200 were taken out of service, and 50 were sent to North's scrapyard at Sherburn-in-Elmet in Yorkshire. A happier fates awaited others, some being reinstated in London, whilst many more were sold for further service elsewhere.

By the early 1980s the rear-open-platform double-decker, complete with conductor, had come to be regarded as an anachronism, a dinosaur from long

ago, rendered extinct by the meteor of OPO. But suddenly, in the free-for-all deregulated era which dawned out in the provinces on 26 October 1986, a bus that could set off as soon as all the passengers were aboard, leaving the conductor to collect fares as it sped on to the next stop, was seen to have an advantage over its slow-loading OPO competitor, and the Routemaster began to appear in some surprising places. Perhaps most remarkable of these was Glasgow, where a substantial fleet of 80 was run by Clydeside, and another 40 in the attractive blue and yellow livery of Kelvin. Clydeside even managed to

Above: RM1000 would be one of the Routemasters sold, before the decade was out, as a result of the Law Lords' legal ruling against the GLC's 'Fares Fair' policy. Not surprisingly it passed into preservation and is seen here in September 1987 at Alresford railway station on the Mid-Hants Railway.

get hold of RML900, adorning it in a livery featuring the celebrated Glasgow cartoon character 'Our Wullie', which took the fancy of my younger sons when we met up with it passing beneath the ornate glass façade of Glasgow Central station during a visit north of the border. Amongst the many other operators to take advantage of the availability of Routemasters were Southampton City Transport, Southend Transport, Burnley & Pendle, United Counties and Stagecoach (then still a relatively minor independent). Other Routemasters took themselves off to foreign parts.

Many of the liveries applied to Routemasters by their new owners enhanced the solidly attractive 1950s-vintage lines of the London exiles. Two of the best were East Yorkshire's dignified navy blue and primrose and Blackpool's crimson lake and white with, in some cases, elaborate lining. In the Lancashire resort Routemasters found themselves sharing road space with trams — something the

Left: In Glasgow Routemasters often found themselves sharing road space with Leyland Nationals, just as they had in London. Clydeside's RM974 is seen in the city centre in October 1988.

earliest examples had missed out on by some half a dozen years in the capital.

Routemasters continued to be sold throughout the 1980s, such that by the end of the decade there were fewer than 300 on LT's books. The RMLs, with their greater capacity, remained virtually intact and were concentrated on the busiest routes serving the City and the West End with the result that virtually every bus passing along Oxford Street was a Routemaster. Fifty Routemasters were transferred early in 1986 to the LT's Wandsworth-based Commercial Operations Unit, subsequently renamed London Coaches; for sightseeing and private-hire duties 20 of these were converted to open-top — a configuration that was to become increasingly popular, and not just in the summer months, as London winters seemed to be getting less severe, heralding what would later be declared as global warming.

Left: Pictured in March 1988, with Blackpool's famous tower as a backdrop, RM848 looks quite splendid in the ornate livery applied by Blackpool Transport. One of 13 Leyland-engined Routemasters to see further service in the Lancashire resort, it got the chance to strike up an acquaintance with trams (something RM1 missed out on by just two years in London), the tracks for which can just be seen on the seaward side of the promenade.

Above: RML2601 on route 12 in Oxford Street — the natural habitat of both bus and route — in the spring of 1986. Based at Peckham garage, it is heading for Notting Hill Gate, a venue which at this time was becoming ever more fashionable, as would later be confirmed by the film starring Hugh Grant and Julia Roberts. *Graham Smith*

Below: RM90 was one of 50 Routemasters which passed in January 1986 to London Buses' Commercial Operations Unit, being one of 20 open-toppers. It is seen here alongside preserved RF672 and an AEC tanker at that year's Cobham Open Day.

Above: Two of the 11 former Green Line Routemaster coaches employed on sightseeing duties, RCL2248 leading, await customers in Lower Regent Street in the spring of 1986.

Right: Still painted red but by now in the service of Midland Red (East), the former DM1747 awaits custom in Leicester's St Margarets bus station in 1982.

The fate of the DM/DMS-class Fleetlines was quite different from — yet, in some respects, parallel to — that of the Routemaster. Many had very short working lives in the capital, yet by the end of the 1980s, 12 years after the last examples had been delivered, there were still some 300 in passenger service in London. Given the abuse heaped upon these unfortunate vehicles and the fact that withdrawal had begun as early as 1978 (just seven years after DMS1 entered passenger service), it is remarkable that that there should have been any at all. In the late 1970s London Transport had declared that the DMS simply wasn't up to the rigours of coping with London conditions, and by the early 1980s sales were in full flow. However, most found ready buyers, many in major conurbations such as Birmingham, Glasgow and Manchester, not to mention the hundreds exported to Hong Kong. The fact is that the DMS, unlike the Merlin and the Swift, was not a bad bus, and with tender loving care it was perfectly capable of working in even the most arduous conditions. Midland Fox, Wilts & Dorset and Maidstone & District were amongst many who bought fleets of second-hand DMSs. It seemed odd to see them passing my front door in Wareham, but they obviously liked the Dorset air, for they lasted a good 10 years, proving to be something of a bargain.

Back in London all Fleetlines other than B20 variants, of which there were 400, had been withdrawn from normal service by the end of 1985.

Withdrawn and sold by LT in 1981, DMS1682 passed to Ensignbus, which, as its own contribution to LT's Golden Jubilee celebrations, repainted the vehicle in a highly effective version of prewar LPTB livery. Renumbered DF1682, the bus was back in Central London in May 1985, being seen on sightseeing duties in Grosvenor Square. Having developed a taste for such work, it later applied for a US visa and had itself shipped across the Atlantic to take up an offer, complete with work permit, from Apple Tours of New York.

Unique to London, the B20 differed significantly from the standard Fleetline and at the rear, as part of its 'quiet bus' specification, featured two 'chimneys' (one on either side of the rear window) which contained the exhaust and air inlets. By the mid-1980s the spread of OPO (and the fact that their unique specification made them less likely to appeal to second-hand buyers) led to a decision to retain and overhaul the B20s, most being re-engined with Iveco units fitted by outside contractors. The type became concentrated in Wandle District in South London (this being the only part of the capital not to have received large numbers of Metrobuses or Titans), where, by the end of the decade, many bore a broad yellow stripe and the legend 'Suttonbus'. The very last one, DMS2438 would be withdrawn from normal service from Croydon (TC) garage in 1993, but the DMS was to remain in use on driver-training and sightseeing work into the 21st century.

Right: Notwithstanding London Transport's desire to rid itself of its Fleetlines as soon as possible, Croydon garage seemed to make a better job than most of operating the type. In 1983, to celebrate the centenary of the town's charter, D2629 was outshopped in a pleasing replication of Croydon Corporation Tramways livery, appearing thus at LT's Golden Jubilee celebrations at Chiswick in July.

Below: Croydon's DMS2286 stands outside Norwood garage late in 1986. By this time the DMSs on the 68 were being replaced by recently delivered Leyland Olympians, one of which (L174) can be seen behind, although one of the former would survive on this busy route to become the last of its type in ordinary service, remaining thus until early 1993.

Left: Proclaiming its allegiance to Suttonbus (a name first applied in November 1988), B20 Fleetline D2640 heads through Kingston in June 1989.

Below: Four of the (by now) relatively rare Fleetlines gather in Sutton in June 1989. On the left is Suttonbus D2615, while on the right, with London General names, is DMS2463.

• 8 •

The London
Regional Transport Act

THE bill which Nicholas Ridley, Secretary of State for Transport, brought before Parliament and which became law on 29 June 1984 paved the way for dramatic changes to public transport in London. Although much was made of 'improving bus and Underground services' and 'making the service more attractive to the public', this was supposed to be achieved whilst the level of revenue support from ratepayers and taxpayers would be halved by 1987/8 compared to 1984/5, the actual figures being £95 million and £192 million respectively.

So how was this extraordinary conjuring trick to be achieved? Key phrases in the Act were 'sale of public assets which are no longer required' and 'smaller and more efficient units'. John Telford-Beasley was appointed Managing Director of London Buses. In his previous post responsible for selling pharmaceuticals in the 'Mediterranean areas of Europe and Africa', and before that managing director of a

company in the Cadbury Schweppes group, he cannot be said to have had a career steeped in public transport, nor had he very much experience of actually using it. However, the fact that his predecessor, Dr David Quarmby, went off to join the board of Sainsbury's, proved that the world had changed greatly since the days of Lord Ashfield and Frank Pick, who fashioned life-long careers giving the citizens of London the finest public transport system in the world. Ridley announced there would be no fare increases in 1984, but the newly created London Regional Transport, along with British Rail, brought them in on 6 January 1985. In fairness this was broadly in line with inflation, which, having five years earlier stood at 12%, was now down to 5%.

January 1985 was also the month in which LRT published its first business plan. The monolithic London Buses would be divided into separate companies, greater productivity would be achieved

Right: London Buslines Daimler Fleetline/Park Royal GHV 33N at Colnbrook on 16 July 1985, three days after the start of the first tranche of seven tendered services. The former DM1033 was one of nine DMs acquired via Ensign for route 81; after spending six years with London Buslines, it passed to the Big Bus Company, of Wimbledon. *Graham Smith*

Left: Tendering brought some most unusual-looking vehicles to London's streets. Leyland Cub C924 DKR, one of a pair taken by Crystals for the 146, lacked even route blinds, the number being applied directly to the bodywork. *Kevin Lane*

by a reduced workforce, one-person operation on buses would increase by 12% in the coming year, whilst there would be no reduction in Underground services; by the end of 1987 OPO would rise to 74%, and by mid-1989 to 90%, although LRT recognised that 100% OPO was 'not yet a realistic prospect in London', meaning that there would still be a role for the Routemaster. In the same year 12 routes were put out to competitive tender, the first of what would become universal practice. London Buses retained just six, operation of the others passing to London Country (two), Eastern National (two), London Buslines and Crystals Coaches of Orpington. None of the routes tendered thus far ventured anywhere near Central London.

The vehicles provided by the new operators varied enormously. Len Wright, trading as London Buslines, used ex-LT DMs, painted bright yellow with brown horizontal bands, on the 81 between Hounslow and Slough, while Crystals Coaches, initially operated a very mixed bunch, including various minibuses, on the 146 between Downe and Bromley North pending delivery of a pair of new Leyland Cubs (shades of the C class of prewar days) with 33-seat HTI Maxeta bodywork. Displayed by all non-London Buses vehicles was a sign featuring a large London roundel accompanied by the words 'LONDON REGIONAL TRANSPORT SERVICE'; later this would be simplified to inform intending passengers — lest they be in any doubt — that this was a '**BUS**'.

Right: Route 275 (Walthamstow-Barkingside) was among the earliest routes put out to tender. 'Running in London for London Regional Transport', Eastern National Bristol VR 3126 heads along Forest Road during 1986. *Graham Smith*

Above: In 1987 Leaside District introduced an attractive livery variation whereby LT red was relieved by a deep white waistband and an even deeper black skirt. Metrobus M1000 is seen freshly repainted on a special service to and from Hertford. *R. J. Waterhouse*

Above right: BL94 (OJD 94R), a Bristol LH with 39-seat ECW bodywork, was one of three delivered in 1977 for the Hillingdon Borough 128 Uxbridge–Rickmansworth service, shows off the revised version of its dedicated livery as it passes through Hillingdon in July 1977. *Graham Smith*

Right: The BLs used on the 128 were withdrawn in July 1988 and replaced by Leyland Nationals, which in turn soon gave way to Leyland Lynxes. LX1 was one of a pair funded by the London Borough of Hillingdon and delivered in December 1988. *Graham Smith*

By now bus travel was beginning to inch its way to a situation where, a decade or so hence, the conductor would become totally redundant, while all the driver would have to do would be to drive; no-one would buy a ticket on the bus itself. One-day passes for inner and outer zones, which could be used after 10.00 Monday-Friday (and all day at weekends) cost £1.10. The newly introduced seven-day, all-zones Capitalcard, which could be used on all British Rail, Underground and London bus services, cost £15 — which, as the *London Bus Magazine* commented, was 'exceptionally good value'. By the middle of 1985 more than half a million passengers were using Travelcards. At the beginning of January 1986 fares went up by around 6.5%, although the increase was less for Travelcards valid for seven days or longer.

In 1986 anti-assault screens were fitted to driver's cabs on 3,500 OPO vehicles. London Buses claimed that, on OPO buses, damage to upper-deck cushions alone was costing £¼ million, prompting it to try out hard, anti-vandal seats. This was fair enough, but certain old fuddy-duddies were inclined to reflect that this was a pastime from which disaffected youth refrained in the days when every bus had a conductor. However, modern technology would come to the rescue when, in 1987, the first video cameras were experimentally installed on six buses. Their success — and the gradual reduction in the cost of fitting them — eventually led to their universal adoption.

At the beginning of 1988 bus and Underground fares rose by 9.5% — almost double the rate of inflation. This was justified on the grounds that, with the popularity of the Underground breaking all records, much investment was needed to improve facilities. In 1989 fares again rose by more than the rate of inflation, as previously to fund the record levels of investment in the Underground but also to cover the 'growing costs of vandalism and graffiti'. These latter were certainly becoming a considerable nuisance, perhaps because, as suggested, society was simply going downhill, but the growth of self-service in shops of every description and the difficulty of removing paint sprayed from aerosol cans certainly were contributing factors. Misguided souls saw graffiti as an art form, and in the USA there were even books published celebrating it; it *could*, in well under 1% of cases, possess artistic merit, brightening up derelict bits of inner suburbs, but it did nothing to enhance the paintwork (to say nothing of the windows) of London's buses and trains. Fortunately it never reached the endemic proportions seen on the New York subway system, although a solution was eventually found there.

Travel for the Disabled, and the Hoppa

FOR those with any kind of disability public transport has always been fraught with difficulties, but it was not until the 1980s that serious consideration was given to addressing the situation, and by 1987 London Regional Transport had a statutory responsibility in this area. Since July 1986 Alder Valley North had been working a service, marketed as Careline, between Heathrow Airport, Victoria Coach Station and various mainline rail termini, using Leyland Nationals converted to accommodate eight wheelchairs as well as 21 seated passengers, but this was not a commercial success. The following year, as a partial replacement, the 24 Metrobuses used on the Airbus service were each equipped with a wheelchair lift, this being fitted in the centre doorway. At around the same time the contract for the remaining Careline services was awarded to London Buses Ltd, which took over in March 1988. Three Optare CityPacers were provided, with room for three wheelchairs and 14 seats. Painted in LT red, with 'Carelink'

prominently displayed, they ran hourly between Liverpool Street, King's Cross, Euston, Paddington, Victoria and Waterloo. The fare was £1, or 50p for holders of disabled permits. It was not a great success and, as the editor of the *London Bus Magazine* commented, 'Disabled people's fears of being stranded at a London terminus, and possibly missing connections, generate strong incentives either not to travel at all or to seek other methods of crossing London.' Eventually European legislation would compel bus companies to find more satisfactory solutions for the less able-bodied, and the decade that followed would see the introduction of ultra-low-floor buses onto which wheelchairs (as well as pushchairs — or 'buggies', as they became known) could be manoeuvred straight from the pavement with relative ease.

Alder Valley North's wheelchair-accessible Leyland National demonstrates its capabilities at Waterloo. *Ian Allan Library*

Providing disabled access to the Underground system is vastly more tricky than fitting out a bus to take wheelchairs. With the tower of Southwark Cathedral as a backdrop, Leyland National LS320, on Mobility Bus route 970, passes London Bridge Underground station in February 1988.

Optare, meanwhile, had risen from the ashes of Charles H. Roe of Leeds and was rapidly finding a niche in the minibus market. Purpose-built and much more comfortable than the original 'bread vans', the CityPacer, based on Volkswagen chassis, was a step ahead of its competitors. In October 1986 CityPacers appeared in the heart of the West End on a new route, C1, which ran from Westminster to Kensington. Named 'Hoppas' (which snappy title soon spread elsewhere), these 25-seaters, classified OV, lived in the basement of Victoria garage. The drivers, both men and women, were hand-picked and were wonderful ambassadors for a service which proved highly popular, and by the end of the decade minibuses and midibuses could be found all over London. In the end they would become victims of their own success, being in most instances replaced by full-sized buses as demand outstripped capacity. In the meantime truck-based vehicles based variously on Iveco, Renault and Mercedes-Benz chassis, as well as the purpose-built MCW Metrorider (which Optare would later take over and develop), all contributed to a scene hugely different from the days of 100%-Chiswick-designed 'big' buses.

Above left: On 25 October 1986 a batch of 19 VW LT55/Optare CityPacer 25-seaters entered service on the prestigious new C1 — Central London's first midibus route — linking the shoppers' mecca of Sloane Square, Knightsbridge and South Kensington with Victoria and Parliament Square. The buses were owned by LRT and operated by London Buses from Victoria garage (GM), while their drivers were selected especially for their patience and friendliness. The service was an instant success. Pursued by a Leyland Titan, OV17 (although it did not carry this designation) passes the Palace of Westminster in March 1988.

Left: OV15 heads west along Buckingham Palace Road in June 1988 as a Maidstone & District 'Invictaway' Duple Laser-bodied Leyland Tiger prepares to turn right into Victoria Coach Station.

Above: Deep in early-20th-century suburbia, 'Kingston Hoppa' MCW Metrorider MR10 heads for Hook on 9 July 1987. *Graham Smith*

Right: MRL129, a Cummins-engined long-wheelbase MCW Metrorider of 1988, passes Tower Hill while on route 100 in June 1989.

• 10 •

The New 'Red Bus' Companies

THE LRT Business Plan for 1988/9 referred to the division of the management of the bus fleet into more than a dozen separate units. In the event there were 11, based loosely on the former district set-up; these were Centrewest, East London, Leaside, London Central, London Forest, London General, London Northern, London United, Metroline, Selkent and South London. This was a prelude to their being sold off into private ownership, which would come about in the early 1990s.

By now, although red remained the basic livery for a London bus, the units within London Buses Ltd were applying all sorts of stripes, bands and logos for various routes. One which certainly caught the eye, not least because it terminated in Trafalgar Square, was an express service (X15) to and from East Beckton inaugurated in March 1989 by East London, using reinstated RMCs fetchingly decked out in red with gold window surrounds and, of course, East London's adopted logo featuring a Thames barge. Centrewest, meanwhile, introduced its U-line network in Uxbridge, with buses suitably adorned, and there was much more in this manner. But all this was merely the prelude to even more dramatic events with the advent of privatisation in the early 1990s. Out in what had been the Country Area it was already happening.

Competitive tendering, which had begun in 1985 with 12 stage-carriage services, was proceeding apace, and by the end of 1989 the number of routes operated in this way covered some 45 million bus-miles, double that of two years earlier.

Right: The Selkent motif displayed on Olympian L263, briefly and rather fancifully named *Conqueror*, of Plumstead garage.
Kevin Lane

Left: The final Routemaster, RML2760, always regarded as something special, heads past St Paul's on its way to Victoria on Sunday 24 May 1987. Note the yellow band above the upper-deck windows indicative of its weekday allocation to route 15.
Ian Allan Library

Above: DMS2287 on night service N87 at Trafalgar Square, 28 October 1989.
R. J. Waterhouse

Right: B20 DMS2252, with London General unit fleetnames, seen from the open top-deck of a sightseeing Routemaster heading down Whitehall in May 1989.

Below: London General marked its inauguration in 1989 as one of the new operating units by painting two Routemasters in traditional London General livery. One of the pair, RM89, took part in the HCVS run to Brighton in May 1990, being seen here passing through the town's northern suburbs ahead of a Green Line Plaxton Paramount-bodied Leyland Tiger on service 773 from Crawley.

Above: London buses, hired by employees and their families, have always ventured to the seaside at weekends. Seen at Southsea in the summer of 1988, having brought a party from Enfield garage, Leaside Metrobus M1248 is, quite properly, resting in the coach park by the funfair. Alongside is preserved Duple Britannia-bodied AEC Reliance 850 ABK, a native of Southsea but by now resident at the Oxford Bus Museum.

Left: Garage closures were the inevitable result of tendering reverses as independent firms undercut LBL time and time again. Hornchurch, which boasted Titans T1-40 inclusive within its walls, closed five days after this photo of T39 was taken in Elm Park on 19 September 1988.
Keith Wood

· 11 ·

The Tube, the King's Cross Fire and the Docklands Light Railway

The memorial to those who died
in the King's Cross fire of 18 November 1987.

MORE than 100,000 passengers passed through King's Cross Underground station during peak hours in 1987. It was served by three Tube lines, the Piccadilly, Northern and Victoria, and the Circle and Hammersmith & City surface lines. Steps led to the surface platforms, escalators to the Tube. In 1987 these latter were made of wooden slats. At 19.36 on 18 November the London Fire Brigade received a call that smoke had been seen coming from one of the Piccadilly Line escalators. The first team arrived in the remarkably short time of six minutes and went into the ticketing hall, from where they could see a fire burning some 20ft down the escalator shaft with 4ft-high flames emerging from the escalator stairs. Passengers were still coming up from the platforms. At first it seemed as if the fire would be containable, but then suddenly, at 19.45, it erupted and spread into the ticket hall. Black smoke poured from the station exits, the ticketing hall became an inferno, and 31 people died. One of these was a fireman, Station Officer Colin Townsley of Soho, who perished trying to rescue a woman passenger in the ticketing hall.

The subsequent enquiry — the longest-running of its kind to date — established that the fire started 'most likely from the discardment [sic] of a lighted match by a passenger leaving the station'. The actual seat of the fire was the machine room beneath the escalator. LT electrician Karl Hoskin was quoted as saying: 'I remember the machine rooms under the escalators throughout the Underground system before the fire used to be disgusting places covered in oil and grease, but within a very short time after the fire they became so clean you could have almost eaten your dinner off the floor!' A commuter, Andrew Pryde, who would normally have

alighted from a Piccadilly Line train at around this time but missed his station on account of being absorbed in the book he was reading, later recalled: 'The thick-hanging smell of the fire lingered in the Tube station passageways for months afterwards.'

The appalling tragedy and its effects not only shocked Londoners but also reverberated worldwide, leading to a tightening of safety measures on many systems. Smoking was prohibited on the Underground, and its wooden escalators were replaced.

The 1980s was a relatively quiet period in terms of new trains and lines for the Tube system. There was one important development, the opening by the Prince and Princess of Wales of the Piccadilly Line station serving Terminal 4 at Heathrow Airport, on 1 April 1986. It had been hoped that the Jubilee Line extension beyond Charing Cross might come about in the 1980s, and the 1983 stock was conceived for its operation. In the event the extension was postponed, but nevertheless 15 trains were ordered from Metro-Cammell for the Jubilee Line. From the side they looked much like the 1973 stock, but they had deeper driving cab windows made of shatterproof glass. Each train was composed of three cars — a driving

The tunnellers extending the Piccadilly Line towards Heathrow join hands to celebrate their breakthrough, 5 April 1984. Services began in 1986. *Ian Allan Library*

motor car at each end, with a trailer between. New features, such as single-leaf doors and the moquette, were the same as that of the surface 'D' stock. The initial batch of 90 cars entered service from August 1983, but in 1986 the upsurge in travel on the Underground prompted an order for an additional 99 cars which were more or less identical to the earlier examples and began to arrive in October 1987. Another result of the increase in travel on the Tube system was the conversion at Acton Works of some Northern Line 1972 units to form seven four-car trains for the Victoria Line. Various other transfers of stock took place in the 1980s, making it possible to take out of service the Bakerloo Line's long-lived, classic 1938 stock.

Meanwhile, one-person-operation was spreading throughout the system, the Piccadilly Line being converted on 31 August 1987 (its 1973 stock being modified accordingly), the Jubilee Line on 28 March 1988, and the Bakerloo Line on 20 November 1989.

Above: A Piccadilly Line train arriving at Heathrow Central. *LTE*

Right: The extension of the Piccadilly Line comprised an anti-clockwise loop, Heathrow Central station being served first and then Terminal 4. *LTE*

Above: A pair of pilot cars from pre-1938 tube stock at Acton Works Open Day, 3 July 1983. These were used to convey old cars around the system as required. *John Glover*

Below: Ruislip depot, 25 November 1986, with 1959 stock on the left and the preserved train of 1938 stock — examples of which worked the Northern Line for some four decades — on the right. *Brian Morrison*

Above: The 1959 stock was the mainstay of the Northern Line for rather longer than anyone would have wished. This train, arriving at Golders Green in July 1989, is on a northbound working. The third tunnel mouth is for the depot headshunt only, the depot itself being out of sight. *John Glover*

Below: The Central Line's branch to Newbury Park leaves the main line to Epping immediately to the north of Leytonstone. Arriving on the main line in April 1987 is a westbound service comprising 1962 stock; the westbound branch trains emerge from the tunnel mouth on the right. *John Glover*

Left: Charing Cross in January 1986, with a Jubilee Line train of 1983 stock waiting to depart for Stanmore. The Jubilee Line platforms at Charing Cross would close in 1999 with the opening of the Jubilee Line Extension to Stratford. *John Glover*

Below: The 1972 stock was very similar to the 1967 stock, albeit configured for crew operation. A train of the Mk 1 version of this stock is seen at Colindale in July 1989. *John Glover*

Right: Even staff uniforms were revised late in the 1980s to reflect the devolution of London Transport's traditional responsibilities to wholly-owned subsidiaries. Displaying 'UNDERGROUND' over the roundel crossbar, the new uniforms were more relaxed and practical than hitherto.
London Underground

Below: Ticketing technology underwent considerable upheaval during the 1980s; this is one of the Westinghouse-manufactured self-service ticket machines phased in from 1987, on which rows of buttons identify each station on the network.
Hawker Siddeley / Westinghouse Cubic

A wonderful initiative for the enthusiast fraternity was unveiled in 1989. Curiously steam on the Underground had outlived that on British Rail, ex-GWR pannier tanks surviving on engineering duties until the summer of 1971. Now it was due to make a comeback. For two weekends in the summer of 1989 preserved Metropolitan Railway 0-4-4T No 1 worked specials between Amersham and Watford High Street. It was accompanied by equally appealing preserved Metropolitan Railway electric locomotive *Sarah Siddons*. In the 1990s 'Steam on the Met' would expand, so that it was possible to observe steam-hauled trains running side by side, north of Harrow,

Preserved former Metropolitan Railway 0-4-4T No 1 attached to a Manchester, Sheffield & Lincolnshire Railway six-wheel carriage of 1890. The MS&LR became the Great Central Railway, which opened its route to Marylebone, London by way of Quainton, Aylesbury and Harrow in 1899. It always had close links with the Metropolitan Railway, sharing its tracks. No 1 is seen at Quainton alongside the Brill branch platform on 26 September 1987. *John Glover*

hauled by a variety of locomotives ranging from a pannier tank to an LNER-designed 'B1' 4-6-0 which would once have hauled expresses out of Marylebone over this very route.

Construction in the vast Docklands complex is still in its early stages as one of the Docklands Light Railway's original two-car units passes a Leyland National heading west in March 1989.

Of rather more relevance to the travelling public but also of much appeal to the enthusiast was the return in the late 1980s of, if not trams *per se*, something closely related — light rail. The tram had been falling out of favour worldwide since the 1920s, but it had certainly not vanished everywhere, Switzerland and Germany, in particular, remaining faithful. By the beginning of the 1980s the wheel, as it so often does, was turning full circle, and the benefits of light rail, whether through city streets or on reserved tracks — or a combination of the two — were once again being appreciated. In the UK, Tyne & Wear had led the way with its Metro system. Although tram-type vehicles were used, there was no street running, and after much research and discussion a similar system was chosen for London's rejuvenated Docklands, immediately east of the Tower.

The area was changing utterly. Previously home to the busiest dock system in the world, with low-cost housing, much of it rented from the local authority, it was now becoming one of vast tower blocks, an airport, shopping malls and highly desirable, state-of-the-art accommodation. Two routes were chosen for the Docklands Light Railway — one from east to west, linking Docklands and the City of London, the other north to south, 'to provide a link from the main residential areas of Northeast London into the proposed employment areas of the Isle of Dogs'.

Above: Negotiating the tramway-like sharp curves possible with light rail, a DLR train from Fenchurch Street swings across the junction between Westferry and West India Quay in March 1989. Unsuitable for working the tunnel extension to the Bank, the 11 original two-car trains built in Germany by LHB would be sold in 1991, returning to Germany, where, after modification, they were put to work in Essen.

The first 11 vehicles, built in Germany by LHB, were delivered, ready for the DLR's opening by HM The Queen in July 1987, although a number of teething troubles delayed its use by the public for a month. The control room was at Poplar, and the cars, a type known as P86 stock, had no drivers, which meant that passengers could sit at the front and have a wonderful view of the spectacular, ever-changing panorama of water and construction all around them, although a driver could take over if necessary; normally a Passenger Service Agent (PSA) was in charge, checking tickets and making sure all was well. Top speed was 50mph, although, with plenty of tramway-type sharp bends and steep gradients, there was little opportunity for this to be reached. Despite not everything running smoothly in the early days, the system rapidly established itself, and soon more passengers were being carried in an *hour* than had been planned for in a day. Ten more cars arrived in 1989 from BREL, so that trains could be formed of two cars rather than one. Although all the original vehicles would soon be replaced, the system would grow and grow, with some wonderful stations, totally modern but with something of the confident air the Victorians put into railway infrastructure.

· 12 ·

Privatisation

IN September 1986 London Country Bus Services, since January 1970 responsible for what had previously been London Transport's Country Area, was split into four. South of the River Thames there was London Country (South East) — soon renamed Kentish Bus — with around 220 buses and coaches and garages at Northfleet, Dunton Green and Dartford. To the west was London Country (South West), with 360 vehicles and garages at Chelsham, Godstone, Crawley, Reigate, Leatherhead, Dorking, Guildford, Addlestone and Staines. North of the river, London Country (North West) possessed around 310 vehicles and garages at Slough, Amersham, Hemel Hempstead

Left: Kentish Bus adopted a completely new and attractive livery which gave no clue to the company's origins. Ex-Strathclyde PTE Alexander-bodied Atlantean 632 heads for Woolwich on 22 February 1988, its new colours nevertheless failing to dispel the impression that it would look far more at home on the streets of Glasgow than in London's southeastern suburbs.

Above: The first new full-size vehicles for Kentish Bus, purchased from dealer stock in the summer of 1988, were five Alexander-bodied Scanias, four of which are seen surrounded by Leyland Nationals inside Dunton Green garage. The Scanias' Newcastle registrations give a clue as to the company's ownership by Proudmutual. *Graham Smith*

and Garston (Watford). Finally, London Country (North East) kept its 340 vehicles in garages at Stevenage, St Albans, Hertford, Hatfield, Harlow and Grays. The National Bus Company had objected to the split, requested by the Government ahead of the planned privatisation of NBC, but there was no diverting Mr Ridley's drive towards 'the development of competition … and the benefits that deregulation is designed to bring'.

Of the new companies only Kentish Bus opted for a complete makeover, adopting an attractive new livery of lemon and maroon. The other three retained green as a basic colour, although London Country (North East) was quick off the mark in introducing new shades. Less than a year later all four companies were put up for sale. London Country (North West) was the subject of a management buyout. London Country (South West) was bought by Drawlane, which also owned Midland Red (North),

Shamrock & Rambler and North Western. London Country (North East) was sold to AJS Holdings, whilst Kentish Bus became the property of Proudmutual, which also owned Northumbria. In the years that followed there would be many more changes of ownership, titles and liveries and the moving of vehicles around the country, so that, for instance, I was able to ride along the cliffs at Whitley Bay in a Northumbria Olympian/ECW coach that had started life on Green Line route 720. Meanwhile, in 1989, the privatised London Country (South West) re-stylted itself as London & Country and introduced an attractive new livery comprising lime and LT-style dark green with a red band — in the opinion of your author one of the most attractive bus liveries of all time. In the same year London Country (North West), which had by now passed to Luton & District control, adopted a darker green and grey.

Above: London Country (North West) Iveco/Robin Hood MB162, working route 350 on 22 October 1988, negotiates the bus-only gate at Headstone Lane, Harrow, activated by the driver's key. *Graham Smith*

Above left: London Country (South West) AN354, a Park Royal-bodied Leyland Atlantean acquired in 1986 from Northern General, poses at Addlestone in its owner's handsome new livery of two-tone green and red.

Left: A varied line-up at West Croydon bus station in September 1989. From left to right are London Country (South West) Leyland National — not a BMW, despite its good effort at such a pretence — SNB209 on the 408 and London Buses MC1 (F430 BOP), a Mercedes-Benz 811D/ Carlyle 28-seat minibus demonstrator, and Olympian L257 (D257 FYM). In the background a London Country (South West) Atlantean works the 403.

The brave new world was not without its drawbacks. In May 1988 London Country (North East) and London Country (North West) were hauled over the coals by the Metropolitan Traffic Commissioner following an increasing number of public complaints over unreliability. Both were banned from registering any new services for six months, and LCNW was censured and was told that it was 'unjustified (and perhaps arrogant) in assuming that the public would prefer the Company's own curtailed and irregular service rather than the possibility of none at all, and also assuming that no other operator could pick up any services they might have discarded'.

Meanwhile, even if deregulation in London was not yet imminent, the process of transferring ownership of the capital's red buses to the private sector was moving inexorably forward. Early in 1988 the Government admitted that parliamentary time would not be available to pass a deregulation bill but anounced that 'deregulation in London during the 1990s is still the Government's intention'. Fierce opposition from a range of expert opinion, coupled with the departure from the scene of both Thatcher and Ridley, helped ensure that the deregulation of London's bus services would, in fact, never come to pass. The advent of privatisation of the bus-owning companies probably really dawned on most Londoners only in late 1988, when one of the most famous of all Central London routes, the 24, was taken over by 30 grey/green-liveried, Alexander-bodied Volvo B10M Citybuses owned by — wait for it — Grey-Green. The route ran from Pimlico, around Parliament Square, along Whitehall,

Late in 1988 the 24 was awarded to Grey-Green, with the result that red buses no longer worked this long-established route. On the plus side it went on to win a competition to find 'Britain's brightest bus service', attracting thousands more passengers and proving much more reliable than hitherto. Grey-Green Volvo B10M/Alexander 122 waits time at one of London's most famous bus termini, below Hampstead Heath.

passing the time with Nelson, and then up through the book- and theatrelands of Charing Cross Road and Cambridge Circus; carrying on to the hi-fi and furniture mecca of Tottenham Court Road, it then exchanged cheery greetings with Humph and the other maniacs at Mornington Crescent before offering to buy or sell anything slightly off-centre at Camden Market and finally terminating in the highly desirable, intellectually stimulating, leafy embrace of Hampstead Heath.

Out in the suburbs the voters were rapidly becoming used to this sort of thing. They were not always best pleased. One object of their displeasure was Harrow Buses, set up as an autonomous unit within London Buses Ltd in November 1987, 'inadequate vehicles' and 'inadequate timetabling' being amongst the more polite comments. A mixed bag of buses, including some ex-Manchester Fleetlines — 'slow and in filthy condition' — in a mixed bag of liveries (and some still carrying advertisements for a superstore in Atherton), were part of the problem, although the later arrival of new Metrobuses heralded better times. They could hardly have been worse.

It did not help that contracts were often awarded to the lowest bidder, which inevitably resulted in the lowest standard of service, provided by poorly paid drivers who were often not up to the job yet had to struggle with badly maintained, unsuitable vehicles and increasingly angry customers.

Right: Among a number of buses acquired second-hand by London Buses in the late 1980s were 50 front-engined Volvo Ailsas that had been new in 1976 to West Midlands PTE. Harrow Buses' V44 makes an impressive sight at South Harrow on 21 November 1987. *Graham Smith*

Below: Harrow Buses came into existence on 14 November 1987. The contrast between hired Northern Counties-bodied Daimler Fleetline YNA 315M (still in the livery of its former operator, Greater Manchester PTE) and new Mk 2 Metrobus M1459, at Harrow Weald garage on 19 December, demonstrates what a very poor impression Harrow Buses made initially. *Graham Smith*

Above: Another of Harrow Buses' hired ex-Greater Manchester Fleetlines, YNA 321M, stops outside Harrow School in December 1987. Were any of the young gentlemen inmates of this top-of-the-range public school bus-spotters? And, if so, what did they make of this rather less than top-of-the-range item of public transport? *Graham Smith*

Above right: Bound for Harrow bus station but without Harrow Buses transfers (or fleet number), recently delivered SR50, a Mercedes-Benz 811D/Optare StarRider seating 26 plus 15 standing (bit of a squash, to say the least) heads through Pinner on 14 October 1989. *Graham Smith*

Right: MCW Metrorider MR28 alongside StarRider SR92 at South Harrow railway station on 14 October 1989, during the MR/SR changeover period. It was around this time also that Optare took over production of Metrorider, re-styling it the MetroRider. *Graham Smith*

Bexleybus 100 (hitherto DMS2121) passes through Dartford in January 1988 on the 96, which replaced trolleybus route 696 in March 1959. Behind is a newly delivered Northern Counties-bodied Leyland Olympian, Bexleybus 14 (a.k.a. L277), while on the left is an older, ECW-bodied Olympian. *Graham Smith*

Bexleybus — another London Buses subsidiary — came into existence in January 1988. Again, joy was not unconditional. Once again a very mixed bag of vehicles was provided, ranging from minibuses of various types and degrees of comfort to — most remarkably — a number of DMSs which had been sold for further service in Scotland some years earlier. A two-day strike two weeks into the new set-up was not well received. Meanwhile the erstwhile Maidstone Corporation, which now styled itself 'Boro'line Maidstone', was assuming an increasingly high profile in London's southeastern suburbs, including the Bexley area, and penetrated right into the West End when it took over the 188, which ran between Greenwich and Euston. Boro'line would eventually become over-ambitious; it lost the 188 in 1990, found itself in debt and was bought

out by Kentish Bus. The connection between Maidstone and what had been the Country Area services in Kent would become closer in the 1990s, these finally being integrated when Maidstone & District (which had moved into the former Corporation garage in the county town) and Kentish Bus both found themselves part of British Bus (later Arriva).

The 1980s ended with huge changes in progress. One of the principal stated intentions of breaking up the National Bus Company, including its operations in what had been the Country Area of London Transport, was that much smaller, locally based firms would emerge, able to respond instantly to changing local needs. It is therefore ironic that eventually the opposite would result, with big groups dominating in a situation reminiscent of the BET/Tilling set-up of earlier times.

Despite subsidies from local authorities, bus travel in many parts of the UK away from cities, towns and conurbations continued to decline. But in London the number of bus and Underground passengers just went on growing. Whatever the merits of London Transport's designing its own vehicles (and quite

Ipswich Buses Roe-bodied Atlantean 94, on hire to Boro'line Maidstone, at the Elephant & Castle on 14 February 1989. The presentation of this 15-year-old vehicle is indicative of the depths to which tendering could sink in its early days. *Graham Smith*

often building them) and maintaining a rigorous overhaul regime at its great works at Chiswick and Aldenham, the world of the 1980s and 1990s demanded something quite different. The last more-or-less purpose-designed London buses — the Merlin and Swift single-deckers and the DMS double-decker — had been a disappointment, while the Titan was expensive and no better than its provincial contemporary, the Metrobus, which fared perfectly well in London.

The future was diversity. For a while it seemed as if even the traditional red livery might vanish, but ultimately the priceless asset of immediate recognition, both by Londoners and by visitors, would see it retained. There would be many owners, but overall control of London's public transport would remain in the hands of a single authority. In the years to come, whilst facing nothing like the devastation of the World War 2 years, the capital's buses and trains would find themselves threatened

by misguided elements bent on destruction. Yet, as London continued to become more and more of a world city, welcoming — usually — incomers from every corner of the globe, as we became ever more aware of the threat of pollution and global warming and the need to control and restrict use of the motor car (despite, many of us, enjoying an ever greater disposable income, on which we might feel tempted to indulge in ever grander private transport — the notorious 'Chelsea Tractor') so common sense, backed up (and sometimes led) by legislation, would ensure that public transport would assume an ever more important role in maintaining a civilised way of life for Londoners and their visitors.

Right: Another bus hired by Boro'line Maidstone was Nottingham City Transport Daimler Fleetline/ Northern Counties 201 of 1976, seen at Euston bus station on 5 December 1988. Its distinctive Nottingham styling and livery looked rather striking, but plastering it with stickers for London service did nothing for the image of route 188. *Graham Smith*

Below: Now this is altogether better. Seen at Aldwych on 30 March 1989 is Boro'line 926, an Alexander-bodied Volvo B10M, one of 14 identical buses delivered a few days earlier. *Graham Smith*